ISBN 978-1-330-71604-5
PIBN 10096167

1 MONTH OF
FREE
READING

at

www.ForgottenBooks.com

By purchasing this book you are eligible for one month membership to ForgottenBooks.com, giving you unlimited access to our entire collection of over 700,000 titles via our web site and mobile apps.

To claim your free month visit: www.forgottenbooks.com/free96167

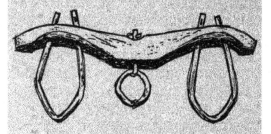

Truths of History

PRESENTED BY

MILDRED LEWIS RUTHERFORD
Athens, Georgia

A FAIR, UNBIASED, IMPARTIAL, UN-PREJUDICED AND CONSCIENTIOUS STUDY OF HISTORY

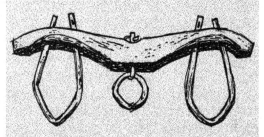

INDEX

The Constitution of the United States (1787) Was a Compact Between Sovereign States and Not Perpetual Nor National.

AUTHORITY:

II.

Secession Was Not Rebellion.

AUTHORITY:

III.

The North Was Responsible for the War Between the States.

AUTHORITY:

IV.

The War Between the States Was Not Fought to Hold the Slaves.

AUTHORITY:

V.

The Slaves Were Not Ill-Treated in the South and the North Was Largely Responsible for Their Presence in the South.

AUTHORITY:

VI.

Coercion Was Not Constitutional.

AUTHORITY:

VII.

The Federal Government Was Responsible for the Andersonville Horrors.

AUTHORITY:

VIII.

The Republican Party That Elected Abraham Lincoln Was Not Friendly to the South.

AUTHORITY:

IX.

The South Desired Peace and Made Every Effort to Obtain It.

AUTHORITY:

X.

The Policy of the Northern Army Was to Destroy Property— That of the Southern Army to Protect It.

AUTHORITY:

CONTRAST:

XI.

The South Has Never Had Her Rightful Place in Literature.

AUTHORITY:

XII.

The North Violated the Constitution and Refused to Stand By the Decisions of the Supreme Court and This Drove the South to Secession.

AUTHORITY:

XIII.

Jefferson Davis Must Have His Rightful Place in History.

AUTHORITY:

XIV.

Abraham Lincoln Must Have His Rightful Place in History.

AUTHORITY:

XV.

Reconstruction Was Not Just to the South—It Made the Ku Klux Klan a Necessity.

AUTHORITY:

XVI.

Race Prejudice is Stronger in the North Than in the South.

AUTHORITY:

XVII.

The South Was More Interested in the Freedom of the Slaves Than the North.

AUTHORITY:

XVIII.

Why the South Demands Corrected Textbooks.

AUTHORITY:

XIX.

The Vilification of Jefferson Davis Became Necessary to Make the Glorification of Abraham Lincoln More Effective.

AUTHORITY:

XX.
Some of the Omissions of History.
AUTHORITY:

INTRODUCTION

The South is not given credit for the part she deserves in the making of the Nation. The text books that are now being used are most unjust to her; the reference books now in the libraries are most unjust to her; the omissions in history as now written are most unjust to her; the history as now written, if accepted, will consign her to infamy.

Realizing this, "THE TRUTHS OF HISTORY" gathered from statements made by men of unquestioned authority, have been put together in a connected way for the guidance of any desiring to have the proofs concerning these facts at hand.

It is hoped that every teacher of history and literature will use "TRUTHS OF HISTORY" in connection with their text books to counteract the falsehoods of history which are now to be found everywhere in literature.

It has been stated that eighty one per cent. of the schools and colleges in the South are today using text books untrue to the South, and seventeen per cent. are using histories omitting most important facts concerning the South.

Dr. J. L. M. Curry, in his *"Southern States of the American Nation,"* says:

> "History, poetry, romance, art, and public opinion have been most unjust to the South. If the true record be given, the South is rich in patriotism, in intellectual force ,in civic and military achievements, in heroism, in honorable and sagacious statesmanship—but if history as now written is accepted it will consign the South to infamy."

The South should not be afraid to speak the truth and call injustice by its proper name. In failing to do this heretofore we have been unjust to the South.

For fear of offending some personal friends of the North, we have assumed an apologetic tone too long; and for fear of failing to secure an office or some honor we have allowed politics to make us unjust.

There is no need for any animus to be shown, for no facts must be stated which cannot be substantiated by reliable authority on the other side—*but we must not be afraid to speak boldly.*

PREFACE

The histories as now written magnify and exalt the New England colonies, and the Mayflower crew with bare mention of Jamestown Colony, thirteen years older, and the crews of the *Susan Constant*, the *Discovery*, and the *Goodspeed*—the names of these vessels are not even given in most histories.

An extended account is always given of the religious faith and practice of the New England Colony, but little or nothing is said of the religious faith and practice of the Jamestown Colony, and no mention of Sir Thomas Dale's Code in the Jamestown Colony—that code which enforced daily attendance upon Divine worship, penalty for absence, penalty for plasphemy, penalty for speaking evil of the Church, and refusing to answer the Catechism, and for neglecting work.

Histories as now written lay great stress upon the industries of the New England colonies, and speak of the South as made up of "a landed aristocracy with slavery as its only excuse for existence."

They speak of slavery as a most barbarous institution, and while holding Virginia responsible for introducing slaves into the American colonies, they say nothing of the slave trade and who was responsible for that. They record that William Penn urged the freedom of the slaves, and do not tell that William Penn died a slaveholder.

They are careful to tell of the great men of New England, which they should do, but they should not make one believe that they alone were responsible for making the Nation great.

While stressing the prominent part taken by their great men, they fail to tell you that many of them stood for State Sovereignty and the right of Secession as strongly as the South did.

They will tell you of the nineteen patriots at Lexington, but overlook entirely the one hundred patriots at Alamance. They will tell you of the Boston Tea Party but ignore the tea parties at Charleston, Annapolis and other Southern ports, and omit the Edenton, (N. C.) tea party where fifty-one patriotic women organized the first patriotic organization for women in the world—"The Daughters of Liberty."

II.

They will tell you of Otis, Samuel Adams, John Adams and other men of New England, but make no mention of Edmund Pendleton, of Virginia, who first suggested that we should be free of English rule, nor of Thomas Nelson, of Virginia, who read Pendleton's Resolutions in the Virginia Assembly, nor of Richard Henry Lee who was sent to the Continental Congress to present these Resolutions, yet these were the Resolutions that were adopted and resulted in the Declaration of Independence that made us a Nation.

They will not tell you that the Executive, Judicial and Legislative branches of the Government were proposed by a Southern man, and that John Marshall of Virginia settled the relations of these to the Government.

They will tell of the great abolition movement, and extol William Lloyd Garrison, Wendell Phillips, John G. Whittier, Walt Whitman, the Beechers and others, but omit to tell you that Washington, George Mason, Thomas Jefferson, John Randolph, James Madison, John Monroe, the Lees and others planned to free their slaves and advocated the colonization or the gradual emancipation of all slaves.

They will tell you that Abraham Lincoln "broke the shackles that bound the poor slaves," but will not tell you that Abraham Lincoln left the poor slaves in non-seceding states still wearing the shackles, and a Southern man, John Brooks Henderson of Missouri, by the Thirteenth Amendment freed them after Lincoln's death.

They will tell you that Liberia was bought by a Benevolent Society "to colonize the poor slaves," but will not tell you that a Southern man was the president of that society, and that the capital of Liberia was named Monrovia after James Monroe of Virginia, and protected by the Monroe Doctrine.

They will tell you of the horrible assassination of Abraham Lincoln, and it was, but say nothing of the far more horrible hanging of Mrs. Surratt, an innocent woman, without judge or jury, upon a false accusation, nor of Dalgren's plan to assassinate Jefferson Davis and his entire Cabinet, and no condemnation followed.

They tell of the falsehood of history, that Jefferson Davis tried to escape in woman's clothes, and say little of the cowardly disguise of Lincoln in entering Washington.

Abraham Lincoln is extolled for continued violations of the Constitution and Jefferson Davis maligned for daring to stand by it and uphold it.

Abraham Lincoln's services to the country are magnified and Jefferson Davis' services to the Federal government minimized.

They will tell you of the horrors of Andersonville, and they were horrors, but fail to tell you who was responsible for them, nor that the mortality was far greater among Southern men in Northern prisons, and without excuse.

The victories of the Northern Army are magnified and the victories of, the Southern Army mentioned lightly or slightingly.

They do not tell that General Grant, a slaveholder, was put as leader. of the Northern Army and General Lee, who had freed his slaves, as the leader of the Southern Army, but they do say that the war was fought to hold the slaves yet do not tell that only 200,000 slaveholders were in the Southern Army, while 315,000 slaveholders were in the Northern Army.

The South is no longer willing to stand for these misrepresentations and omissions of history, and a fair-minded North will not blame the South, and will be ready to hear her side of the story, provided it is given from facts and not traditions.

GENERAL LEE said:

> "Every one should do all in his power to collect and disseminate the truth, in the hope that it may find a place in history and descend to posterity."

Again General Lee said:

> "History is not the relation of campaigns, and battles, and generals or other individuals, but that which shows the principles for which the South contended and which justified her struggle for those principles."

General Lee showed he was far more concerned that the cause should be vindicated than that he should be glorified or any act of his or others be magnified.

He said also:

> "All that the South has ever asked or desired is that the Union founded by our forefathers should be preserved, and that the government as was originally organized should be administered in purity and truth."

BENJAMIN H. HILL felt great concern about this question. He said:

> "We owe it to our dead, to our living, and to our chil-

IV.

dren to preserve the truth and repel the falsehoods, so that
we may secure just judgment from the only tribunal before which we may appear and be fully and fairly heard,
and that tribunal is the bar of history.''

Had the South followed this advice we would not today, after
sixty or more years have passed, be obliged to correct these falsehoods of history. Falsehoods circulated not only in our own
country, but now widely circulated in foreign countries by such
writers as George Creel, Booth Tarkington and Dr. Crane.

THOMAS NELSON PAGE, several years ago, gave the South a great
warning which we of the South did not heed. He said:

> ''In a few years there will be no South to demand a his-
> tory if we leave history as it is now written. How do we
> stand today in the eyes of the world? We are esteemed
> 'ignorant, illiterate, cruel, semi-barbarous, a race sunken
> in brutality and vice,' a race of slave drivers who 'disrupted
> the Union in order to perpetuate human slavery' and 'who
> as a people have contributed nothing to the advancement
> of mankind.' ''

Dr. J. L. M. Curry also warned us. The Confederate Veterans have through their historians, over and over again, warned
us. Colonel Louis Guion in 1900 at New Orleans, La., offered
resolutions providing for history committees to be appointed to
investigate the text books then being used in our schools. The
movement started and several objectionable text books were
ruled out. Other U. C. V. historians did the same. In Col.
Guion's speech before that Convention, he called attention to the
fact that in nearly every history then in use the children were
being taught that their fathers and grandfathers were ''traitors
and rebels,'' and that the war was a war of rebellion and they
were calling it a Civil War. That the children in their literary
work in schools were reciting ''Barbara Frietchie,'' a myth of
history by Whittier's own acknowledgment, and were being
taught that Stonewall Jackson was a Hun in spirit. Also that
they were reciting ''Sheridan's Ride'' by Buchanan Read, who
in the poem alludes to the Confederates as ''traitors.''

I have always found the fair-minded men and women of the
North anxious to hear the South's side of history. I am sure
they have no respect for us when we are afraid to tell the truth.

The South has really more to fear from the omissions of history than from falsehoods included in the text books now writ-

ten. One of the greatest omissions is the heroic part the men in the Southern Navy took in the War between the States.

When the news reached them that Fort Sumter had been fired upon, they from a high-toned sense of honor surrendered their vessels to the United States Government from whom they had received their commission, and then returned home to cast in their lot with their own states. This sacrifice was a great one and meant giving up all that they had received in education, training for the Navy and in the experience they had gained in service. It meant foregoing all hope of promotion of honors in that line—but they willingly did it for the principle so dear to them. They returned to find the South without a navy and without means then of securing one. They did their best with the vessels available and never murmured. History exalts those Southern men who refused to make this sacrifice and remained in the United States Navy, but omits to tell the heroic deeds of those who under the most trying circumstances won immortal renown. History should be made to record the heroic deeds of the South as well as of the North.

Surely the man who organized the United States Naval Academy at Annapolis, the man who assisted in the capture of Vera Cruz, the man who commanded Perry's flagship in Japan expedition and the man who was placed in command of the Navy Yard at Washington—to say nothing of that man's services in the Confederate Navy, winning the highest honors ever given, being the only one to hold the high office of Admiral, deserves a prominent place in the United States history. Yet one rarely finds the name of Admiral Franklin Buchanan mentioned except in books by Southern men.

Rear-Admiral Raphael Semmes should hold a high place in truthful history not only for his book, *"Service Afloat,"* but ranking as Commander of the *"Alabama"* with John Paul Jones, Decatur, Lawrence, Farragut, Dewey and other great naval heroes, and yet we rarely find his name or his deeds mentioned in history outside of his native state.

The name of Matthew Fontaine Maury, the one who suggested organizing the Naval Academy at Annapolis, the one who wrote the text book for the United States Navy; the one who revolutionized the sailing of the world by charts (the voyage around Cape Horn being shortened by forty days and at a saving to the

Government of $40,000,000 annually); the one who suggested the Weather Bureau, and really was the one responsible for the National Observatory; the one who made Cyrus Field's Atlantic Cable a possibility; the one who redeemed the lands of the Mississippi; the one who established the great circuit routes for ocean steamers; the one who traced the great Gulf Stream— this man of science cannot be left out of truthful history. His name is not even found in the Congressional Library's list of noted scientists because he cast his lot with the Confederate Cause.

Maury was invited to become a member of every leading literary and scientific society in England and on the Continent; he was knighted by Russia, Denmark, Portugal, Belgium, and France. Gold medals were bestowed upon him by Prussia, Australia ,Sweden, Holland, Sardinia, Bremen and France. Germany gave him the *"Cosmos Medal,"* the only duplicate ever given. Cambridge University, England, gave him the degree of LL.D., and Berlin erected a monument to him with this inscription: *"A man whom kings delight to honor,"* and yet his own United States people, because he fought for the South, had his name erased from his wonderful charts, and refused to let him be classed with the great men of science.

Shall omissions as these in history in justice to the world be allowed any longer?

Had the cause of the South in 1865 prevailed, history would have been truthfully written by unprejudiced historians The Southern statesmen who had been true to the Constitution could better have steered the *"Ship of State"* than such men as Thad Stevens, Chas. Sumner, Fessenden, Turnbull, Andrew Johnson and others.

It has taken the South many years to get off of that *"Rock of Offense,"* the Reconstruction Period. While the South was combatting the destructive forces at work during this time—homes were being destroyed, domestic relations were being upset, property was being confiscated, politics was being corrupted, liberty of speech, and liberty of the press were being suppressed—the North was writing the history unmolested and we of the South have allowed this history written from the Northern viewpoint, with absolute ignorance of the South, to be taught in our schools all these years with an indifference that is truly appalling.

We have allowed our leaders and our soldiers to be spoken of as "rebels." Secession was not rebellion.

We have allowed them to be called "traitors"—they could never convict one Southern man for the stand he took in 1861.

We have allowed our cause to be spoken of as a "Lost Cause." The Cause for which the Confederate soldier fought was not a "Lost Cause." The late war was fought to maintain the very same principle—*the non-interference with just rights.* The trouble in 1865 was that the South failed to maintain this principle by force of arms. Being a Republic of Sovereign States and not a Nation she had the right to resent any interference with rights which had been guaranteed to her by the Constitution. The South never has abandoned the principle for which she fought nor ever will. By overwhelming arms, 2,850,000 to a small handful, comparatively speaking, 600,000, she was forced to surrender, and in surrendering she was forced to submit to the terms of parole which were that she should never secede again. This does not mean that the right to secede is not still in the Constitution, but the promise has been made never to try it again, and she will keep that promise.

We have allowed the war to be called a Civil War, because the North called it so when history was first written, and by allowing this we acknowledged that we were a Nation, not Sovereign States, and therefore had no right to secede. No wonder that the doctrine of State Rights has been so misunderstood!

It is with no thought of stirring up sectional strife, but rather with the desire of allaying sectional bitterness that I am anxious to have the truth known. If the North does not know the South's side of history—and how can she know it if we do not tell it to the world—then the historians of the future will continue to misrepresent the South, and the South will continue to resent the misrepresentations.

We of the South are not advocating the adoption of any one text book, but we are advocating that those text books unjust to the South shall be ruled out of our schools, out of our homes, out of our public and private libraries, and that new encyclopedias and books of reference now being sold or given as a bribe to secure commendation be carefully examined before placed in public or private libraries.

The great underlying thought which animated the soldiers of

VIII.

the Confederacy was their profound regard for the principle of State self-government—they were not fighting to hold their slaves. Only a very small minority of the men who fought in the Southern army were slaveholders.

> "It was the abolitionists of the North who looked on the Constitution of the United States as a 'scrap of paper,' 'a covenant with death and a league with hell,' who demanded an anti-slavery Constitution, an anti-slavery Bible, and an anti-slavery God."

George Lunt, in his *"Origin of the Late War,"* says that such men at the North were in the minority.

The movements for emancipation began early in the South and were hindered by the intemperate and fanatical abuse of slaveholders by the abolitionists and also by the difficult problem of how to regulate the relations of the two races so radically different after emancipation. The South fought for the right to settle her own domestic affairs, free from any interference on the part of self--constituted advisers.

The doctrine of States Rights is not well understood. The States do not derive their rights from the Constitution, but the Constitution derives its rights from the States.

The States do not derive their rights from the Federal Government, but each State derives its power from the people of the State. At last the people hold the power, and it is not the people of all States collectively, but the people of each one of the Thirteen Sovereign States, separately, who act in convention representing the will of the people, so the people must not surrender this power to direct their local affairs to the Government.

GEORGE BANCROFT'S *"History of the United States":*

> "The Federal Government is only a common agent for the transaction of the business delegated to it by the action of the States."

It is not well understood what are the States Rights that are guaranteed by the Constitution.

CHIEF JUSTICE DAY, of the United States Supreme Court, June 3, 1918, said:

> "If Congress can regulate matters entrusted to local authority, the power of the States may be eliminated, and thus our system of government be practically destroyed."

PRESIDENT GROVER CLEVELAND said:

"The doctrine of home rule, as I understand it, lies at the foundation of republican institutions, and cannot be too strongly insisted upon."

THOMAS JEFFERSON said:

"When all government, domestic and foreign, in little things as in great things, shall be drawn to Washington as the center of all power, it will render powerless the checks provided by our government on another, and will become venal and oppressive as the government from which we have just separated."

"Life of Webster," in American Statesmen Series, by Henry Cabot Lodge, Senator from Massachusetts:

"When the Constitution was adopted by the votes of States at Philadelphia, and accepted by the votes of States in popular conventions, it is safe to say that there was not a man in the country, from Washington and Hamilton, on the one side, to George Clinton and George Mason on the other, who regarded the new system as anything but an experiment entered upon as States, and from which each and every State had the right peaceably to withdraw, a right which was very likely to be exercised."

GEORGE CLINTON of New York, said:

"The sovereignty of the States, I consider the only stable security for the liberties of the people against the encroachment of power."

RAWLE'S "View of the Constitution":

"The Union was formed by the voluntary agreement of the States, and in uniting together they have not forfeited their nationality, nor have they been reduced to one and the same people. If one of the States chooses to withdraw its name from the contract, it would be difficult to disprove its right of doing so, and the Federal Government would have no means of maintaining its claim, either by force or right."

The South has been very patient, but can afford to be patient no longer—she must demand that the truth be told, and the truth is all she asks.

She desires that the truth be told in such a way that peace between the sections shall be the result. Peace cannot come until the truth is known and acknowledged by both North and South. These "TRUTHS OF HISTORY" are presented with this thought in mind.

X.

General Bennett H. Young said:

"The time has come when men may speak freely, kindly, and truly of the past. The War between the States with its sacrifices has ceased, and peace between the sections with its ennobling, refining and uplifting influences has come to abide forever. They who would stay its marches and delay its reign are the enemies of the Nation's happiness."

The South should be as quick to resent an injustice to the North in history as she now resents an injustice to the South by the North.

Already instances have come to notice where text books making false statements about the North have been rejected in Southern schools. Will not the North be as magnanimous?

Read *"The Measuring Rod"* for testing text-books, and endorsing books for libraries, which was prepared at the request of the Confederate Veterans. Read the "Warning" given.

MILDRED LEWIS RUTHERFORD.

The Villa, Athens, Ga.

THE TRUTHS OF HISTORY

I.

THE CONSTITUTION OF THE UNITED STATES 1787, WAS A COMPACT BETWEEN SOVEREIGN STATES, AND WAS NOT PERPETUAL NOR NATIONAL.

AUTHORITY:

ELLIOTT'S DEBATES, Vol. V., p. 214:

"When the Constitution was outlined and read, the words *Perpetual Union* which had been in the *Articles of Confederation* were omitted. Alexander Hamilton and others noticing it, and desiring a Union, opposed the adoption of the Constitution. Some one moved to have it made a *National Government*, but this motion was unanimously defeated. Senator Ellsworth of Connecticut and Senator Gorham of Massachusetts have testified to this."

DANIEL WEBSTER, "*The Federalist*," p. 908:

"If the states were not left to leave the Union when their rights were interfered with, the government would have been National, but the Convention refused to baptize it by that name."

DANIEL WEBSTER, *Capon Springs Speech*, in 1851:

"The Union is a Union of States founded upon Compact. How is it to be supposed that when different parties enter into a compact for certain purposes either can disregard one provision of it and expect others to observe the rest?

"If the Northern States wilfully and deliberately refuse to carry out their part of the Constitution, the South would be no longer bound to keep the compact.

"A bargain broken on one side is broken on all sides."

DANIEL WEBSTER in 1833 said:

"If a contract, it rests on plighted faith, and the mode of redress would be to declare the whole void. States may secede if a League or Compact."

HENRY CABOT LODGE says:

"The weak place in Webster's armour in the Hayne-Webster Debate was historical—the facts were against him. And Chief Justice Story in that controversy never once mentioned secession, he was only stressing nullification."

COMMENTARIES ON THE CONSTITUTION, Vol. III, p. 287:

"The attributes of sovereignty are now enjoyed by every State in the Union."—*Alexander Hamilton*.

"The Thirteen States are Thirteen Sovereignties."—*James Wilson* of Pennsylvania.

"Each State enjoys sovereign power."—*Gouverneur Morris*.

"The Government was made by a number of Sovereign States."—*Roger Sherman*.

"The Thirteen States are Thirteen Sovereign bodies."—*Oliver Ellsworth*.

"The States are Nations."—*Daniel Webster*.

Every one of these men were delegates to the Constitutional Convention except Daniel Webster.

THE FEDERALIST, Chapter VIII, Nos. XI, XXXIX:

"If it were a consolidated government the assent of a majority of the people would be sufficient to establish it. but it is to be binding on the people of each State, and only by their own separate consent."

ALEXANDER HAMILTON, *"The Federalist,"* Vol. LX.:

"If the Constitution is adopted (and it was) the Union will be in fact and in theory an association of States or a Confederacy."

DANIEL WEBSTER, *U. S. Senate,* Feb. 15, 1833:

"If the Union was formed by the accession of States then the Union may be dissolved by the secession of States."

BENJAMIN FRANKLIN, *Franklin Works,* Vol. V., p. 409:

"The States acceded to the Constitution."

JUDGE STORY:

"If the Constitution is a compact then the States have a right to secede."

GEORGE BANCROFT, *History of the United States:*

"The States that gave life to the Union are necessary to the continuance of that life."

JAMES BUCHANAN:

"Rawle taught at West Point that the Union was an asociation of independent republics."

CHARLES FRANCIS ADAMS, *"Constitutional Ethics of Secession,"* pp. 16, 17:

"William Rawle was an eminent Philadelphia lawyer and was twenty-nine years of age when the Constitution was adopted. He was, for many years, Chancellor of the Law Association of Philadelphia and principal author of. the revised Code of Pennsylvania, and stood in the foremost rank of the legal luminaries of the first third of the century."

GEORGE BANCROFT says:

"The Constitution was adopted first by States in Convention, each State acting for itself in its own sovereign capacity."

LORD BROUGHAM said:

"The devising of means for keeping its integrity as a federacy, while the rights and powers of the individual States are maintained entire, is the greatest refinement of social policy to which any age has ever given birth."

II.

Secession Was Not Rebellion

AUTHORITY:

DR. HENRY WADE ROGERS, Dean of the Law Department of Yale:

"When peace came it was found that the Articles of Confederation were weak, in that the Central government could not legally assume sovereign power—that power resided in those free, sovereign and independent States, and there was no delegation of any rights to a central head.

"It became necessary, therefore, to change the Articles of Confederation so that the States should be brought to coöperate, by realizing that the government should not be a *perpetual Union*, but an *agreement* by which certain rights were reserved for the Federal government, and certain rights were reserved for the State."

RAWLE'S *"View of the Constitution"* was a text-book used at West Point. Rawle said:

"It will depend upon the State itself whether it will continue a member of the Union."

"If the States are interfered with they may wholly withdraw from the Union." (pp. 289, 290).

"General Lee told Bishop Wilmer, of Louisiana, that if it had not been for the instruction received from Rawle's text-book at West Point he would not have left the United States Army and joined the Confederate Army at the breaking out of the War between the States."

BENJAMIN T. WADE, Senator from Ohio, 1858:

"Who is to be the final arbiter—the government or the States—why, to yield the right of the States to protect its own citizens would consolidate this government into a miserable despotism."

GOLDWIN SMITH of Cornell University:

"The Southern leaders ought not to have been treated as rebels—secession is not rebellion."

JUDGE BLACK, of Pennsylvania, said:

"John Quincy Adams, in 1839, and Abraham Lincoln, 1847, made elaborate arguments in favor of *the legal right of a State to Secede."—Black's Essays.*

AMERICAN CONFLICT, *Horace Greeley,* Vol. I, p. 359:

"Let the people be told why they wish to break up the *Confederation,* and let the act of secession be the echo of an unmistakable popular fiat. Then those who rush to carnage to try to defeat it would place themselves clearly in the wrong."

Again Horace Greeley said:

"If the Declaration of Independence justified the secession of 3,000,000 colonists in 1776, I do not see why the Constitution ratified by the same men should not justify the secession of 5,000,000 of the Southerners from the Federal Union in 1861."—*New York Tribune.*

Again he says:

"We have repeatedly said, and we once more insist that the great principle embodied by Jefferson in the Declaration of Independence that government derives its power from the consent of the governed is sound and just, then if the Cotton States, the Gulf States or any other States choose to form an independent nation they have a clear right to do it."

ABRAHAM LINCOLN said:

"Any people whatever have a right to abolish the existing government and form a new one that suits them better."
—*Congressional Records,* 1847).

GEORGE LUNT, of Massachusetts, says:

"Had Buchanan in 1860 sent an armed force to prevent the nullification of the Fugitive Slave Law, as Andrew

Jackson threatened to do in 1833, there would have been a secession of fifteen Northern States instead of thirteen Southern States."—*Origin of Late War.*

BENJAMIN J. WILLIAMS, of Lowell, Mass., in his book, *Died For Their State,* said:

"In the celebrated resolutions of 1789, Mr. Madison and Mr. Jefferson declared that each State had an equal right to be its own judge. If so, then, the right of secession by the South could have followed, and each State has the right to judge if the infraction is sufficient to warrant her withdrawal."

The Ordinance of Secession was simply the States resuming their delegated sovereign powers in order to organize a Union that would stand by the Constitution. That they had the right to do this, see Hallam's *"Constitutional History of England,"* Vol. II., p. 219.

ABRAHAM LINCOLN said:

"Any people that can may revolutionize and make their own of so much of the territory as they inhabit."—*Appendix* to *Congressional Globe,* 30th Congress, p. 94.

C. W. COTTOM, in a letter to Secretary of Treasury, Howell Cobb in 1860, said:

"The action of the Southern States in seceding from a Union which refused to recognize and protect their Constitutional rights meets with my most cordial approbation."

LUNT's *"Origin of the Late War,"* p. 435, says that in a letter sent to Fanueil Hall, Mr. Everett said:

"If our sister States must leave us, in the name of Heaven let them go in peace."

GEORGE LUNT, *in his "Origin of the Late War,"* (D. Appleton & Co.):

"Had the Democrats won out in 1860 the Northern States would have been the seceding States not the Southern."

EDWARD EVERETT HALE, in his *"Life of William Seward,"* says:

"The Civil War will not be treated as a rebellion, but as a *great event in the history of our nation* which, after forty years, it is clearly recognized to have been."

HORACE GREELEY:

"The right to secede may be a revolutionary one, but it exists nevertheless; and we do not see how one party can have a right to do what another party has a right to pre-

vent. We must ever resist the asserted right of any State
to remain in the Union and nullify or defy the laws there-
of; to withdraw from the Union is another matter. And
when a section of our Union resolves to go out, we shall
resist any coercive acts to keep it in. We hope never to
live in a Republic where one section is pinned to the other
section by bayonets."—*New York Tribune.*

IN THE REPUBLICAN PLATFORM that elected Abraham Lincoln is
found:

"The inviolable rights of each State to order and control
its own domestic institutions.".

CHARLES BEECHER STOWE, the son of Harriet Beecher Stowe,
said:

"When the South drew the sword to defend the doctrine
of States Rights and the institution of slavery, they certainly had on their side the Constitution and the laws of
the land for the National Constitution justified the doctrine of States Rights."

Again, CHARLES BEECHER STOWE said:

"Is it not perfectly evident that there was a great rebellion, but the rebels were the men of the North, and the
men who defended the Constitution were the men of the
South, for they defended States Rights and slavery, which
were distinctly entrenched within the Constitution."

Timothy Pickering, of Massachusetts, was the first to threaten
secession.

Josiah Quincy, of Massachusetts, was the first to mention secession in Congressional Halls—1811.

John Quincy Adams, of Massachusetts, was the first to peti-
tion Congress to dissolve the Union.

Charles Francis Adams testified that there was no doubt but
that his grandfather, John Quincy Adams, believed that a State
had the right to secede.

NEW YORK HERALD, Nov. 11, 1860:

"The South has an undeniable right to secede from the
Union. In the event of secession, the City of New York,
and the State of New Jersey, and very likely Connecticut
will separate from New England when the black man is put
on a pinnacle above the white."

GEORGE LUNT'S *"Origin of the Late War"*:

"Despairing of their rights in the Union, the Southern
leaders advised the Southern States to throw themselves

back on their reserved rights and withdraw from the Union —but it was too late.

"This could have been done in 1850 but not in 1861.

"No State has been more conspicuous in pressing the claims of State Rights from the earliest period than Massachusetts."

GEORGE LUNT:

"The maintenance of the authority of the Stats over matters purely local is as essential to the preservation of our institutions as is the conservation of the supremacy of the Federal power in all matters entrusted to the nation by the Federal Constitution.

"The power of the States to regulate their purely internal affairs of such laws as seem wise to the local authority is inherent and has never been surrendered to the general government."

CHIEF JUSTICE DAY, in a Decision of the U. S. Supreme Court, June 3, 1918:

"If Congress can regulate matters entrusted to local authority, the power of the States may be eliminated and thus our system of government be practically destroyed."

III.

The North Was Responsible for the War Between the States

AUTHORITY:

THE NEW YORK HERALD, April 7, 1861:

"Unless Mr. Lincoln's administration makes the first demonstration and attack, President Davis says there will be no bloodshed. With Mr. Lincoln's administration, therefore, rests the responsibility of precipitating a collision, and the fearful evils of protracted war."

THE NEW YORK HERALD, April 5, 1861:

"We have no doubt Mr. Lincoln wants the Cabinet at Montgomery to take the initiative by capturing two forts in its waters, for it would give him the opportunity of throwing the responsibility of commencing hostilities. But the country and posterity will hold him just as responsible as if he struck the first blow."

SHEPPARD'S "Life of Lincoln":

"Please present my compliments to General Scott and tell him confidentially to be prepared to hold or retake the forts as the case may require after my inauguration."— Abraham Lincoln.

HORTON'S HISTORY, p. 71:

"The withdrawal of the Southern States from the Union was in no sense a declaration of war upon the Federal government but the Federal government declared war on them, as history will show."

GIDEON WELLES:

"There was not a man in the Cabinet that did not know that an attempt to reinforce Sumter would be the first blow of the war."

SEWARD said:

"Even preparation to reinforce will precipitate war."

STEPHEN DOUGLAS said:

"Lincoln is trying to plunge the country into a cruel war as the surest means of destroying the Union upon the plea of enforcing the laws and protecting public property."

ZACK CHANDLER wrote to Governor Blair:

"The manufacturing States think a war will be awful, but without a little blood-letting the Union will not be worth a curse."

GOVERNOR MOORE, of Alabama (Cousin & Hill, p. 371), says:

"I have had a conference with Secretary Mallory, of Florida, and Secretary Fitzpatrick, of Alabama, in which they informed me that they and Secretary Sidell had a personal interview with the President and the Secretary of Navy and were assured by them that no attack would be made upon Fort Sumter and Fort Pickens or any excuse given for the shedding of blood during the present administration."

GENERAL BRAGG (O. R. I., p. 457), says:

"They have placed an engineer officer at Fort Pickens to violate, as I consider, our agreement not to reinforce. I do not believe that we are entirely absolved from all agreement of January 29."

HORTON'S HISTORY, p. 109:

"The first gun of the war was the gun put into that war fleet that sailed against Charleston. The first gun fired at Fort Sumter was the first gun in self-defense. This is the simple fact stripped of all nonsensical with which it has been surrounded by Abolitionists."

HOSMER, "History of the American Nation," Vol. XX, p. 20:

"The determination expressed by Lincoln in his Inaugural Address to hold, occupy and possess the property and places belonging to the United States precipitated the outbreak, and his determination to collect duties and imports was practically an announcement of an offensive war.''

WILLIAM SEWARD said:

"The attempt to reinforce Sumter will provoke war. The very preparation of such an expedition will precipitate war. I would instruct Anderson to return from Sumter.''

J. G. HOLLAND'S *"Life of Lincoln"*:

"Up to the fall of Sumter Lincoln had no basis for action in the public feeling. After the fall of Sumter he could act.'

"Most of Lincoln's ministers were against the reinforcement of Fort Sumter.''

MEDILL, of the *Chicago Tribune*, says:

"In 1864 when the call for extra troops came Chicago revolted. Chicago had sent 22,000 and was drained. There were no young men to go, no aliens, except what was already bought. The citizens held a mass meeting and appointed three men of whom I (Medill) was one to go to Washington and ask Stanton to give Cook County a new enrollment. He refused. Then we went to President Lincoln. 'I cannot do it,' said Lincoln, 'but I will go with you to Stanton and hear the arguments on both sides.'

"So we went over to the War Department together. Stanton and General Frye were there and they both contended that the quota should not be changed. The argument went on for some time, and was finally referred to Lincoln who had been silently listening. When appealed to, Lincoln turned to us with a black and frowning face: 'Gentlemen,' he said, with a voice full of bitterness, 'after Boston, Chicago has been the chief instrument in bringing this war on the country. The Northwest opposed the South, as New England opposed the South. It is you, Medill, who is largely responsible for making blood flow as it has. You called for war until you had it. *I have given it to you.* What you have asked for you have had. Now you come here begging to be let off from the call for more men, which I have made to carry on the war you demanded. You ought to be ashamed of yourselves. Go home and raise your 6,000 men.''—Tarbell's *"Life of Lincoln,"* Vol. II., p. 144.

THE NEW YORK EXPRESS, April 15, 1861, said:

"The people petitioned and pleaded, begged and implored Lincoln and Seward to be heard before matters were brought to a blood extreme, but their petitions were spurned and treated with contempt.''

In *"The Opening of the Twentieth Century"* these words are found:

"The war was inaugurated by the North, and defended on an unconstitutional basis."

Hallam's *"Constitutional History"*:

"The aggressor in war is not the first who uses force, but the first who renders force necessary."

Benjamin Williams, of Lowell, Massachusetts, said:

"The South was invaded and a war of subjugation was begun by the Federal government against the seceding States in amazing disregard of the foundation principle of its existence—and the South accepts the contest forced upon her with a courage characteristic of this proud-spirited people.

"The North had no Constitutional right to hold Fort Sumter in case the States seceded and to hold it meant war."

Horton, pp. 71, 72:

"The forts in the South were partnership property; and each State was an equal party in ownership. The Federal government was only a general agent of the real partners—the States—which composed the Union. The forts were designed to protect the States, and in case of withdrawal of a State the forts went with the State.

"South Carolina could not deprive New York of her forts, nor could New York deprive South Carolina of hers. The seceding States were perfectly willing to settle matters in a friendly way. They were striving only to resume the powers they had delegated."

Senator Joseph Lane, of Oregon, in reply to Andrew Johnson in regard to the Crittenden Resolution (*Congressional Globe,* 36th Congress, p. 1347), said:

"If there is, as I contend, a right for secession, then whenever a State exercises that right this Government has no laws to execute in that State, nor has it any property in such State that can be protected by the power of that Government."

John Codman Ropes, in his *"Story of the Civil War,"* says:

"The South claimed that she had the right to demand the forts, arsenals and government property in her States—these were her sovereign rights. If South Carolina had this sovereign right to demand the surrender of the fort within her jurisdiction, and it belonged to South Carolina as soon as she resumed her sovereign right, then President Lincoln had no right to hold it against her demand—nor to arm or provision it by force. The U. S. Government could not have erected it on South Carolina's soil without South Carolina's consent, and the action of Lincoln was that of centralized despotism. Governor Pickens sent I. W. Hayne, the Attorney General of South Carolina, to President Buchanan saying that the fort was necessary for the protection of the State it was erected to protect—and that South Carolina was willing to pay a full valuation in settlement between the State and the government."

JOHN CODMAN ROPES, in his "Story of the Civil War," pp. 17, 18, again says:

"The States which seceded held, it must be remembered, the theory that the United States was not a single nation, but a collection of nations, which had for many years acted for certain purposes through an agency known as the Government of the United States. To this government tracts of land had been ceded by the different States, that on them might be erected light-houses, forts, arsenals, court-houses, post offices, and the like, all subserving the general welfare, and particularly, that of the State making the cession. These buildings had all been erected at the public expense, and by the general government. The munitions of war, the money, the public property, contained in them belonged to the general government as the agent of all the States united. They were, so to speak, partnership property, and the title to this property stood in the name of the agent of all the parties belonging to the firm.

"If this view of the matter had been accepted, and the right of the State to secede had been conceded there is no doubt that it would have been generally granted that the forts, arsenals, post offices and other public buildings lying within the State which withdrew from the Union ought to have been turned over to that State.

"The South knowing she had the right to secede took this view of the question and seized the property."

WENDELL PHILLIPS said:

"Here are a series of States girding the Gulf which think they should have an independent government: they have the right to decide this question without appealing to you or to me.

"Let the South go! Let her go with flags flying and trumpets blowing! Give her her forts, her arsenals, and her sub-treasuries. Speed the parting guest! All hail dominion! Beautiful on the mountains are the feet of them who bring the glad tidings of disunion."

SENATOR LANE, again says:

"No, Sir, the policy of this government is to inveigle the people of the North into civil war by making the design in smooth and ambiguous terms."

GEORGE LUNT says:

"The Relief Squadron which was twenty-three days getting ready at Norfolk (while the peace commissioners were kept waiting in Washington) bore the aspect certainly of a manoeuvre, which military persons denominate 'stealing a march!' "

"History will record that the woes and sacrifices caused by the war might have been saved by a little manliness on the part of the Republican leaders at this time."

GEORGE LUNT, "*Origin of Late War*," p. 485:

"The external aspect of the affair off Charleston which precipitated the war is that of a boy 'spoiling for a fight' who places a chip on the rim of his hat, and dares his competitor to knock it off."

PERCY GREGG, p. 158:

"The Government was bound in honor to hand over to the seceding States their fair share of armaments created at common expense."

GEORGE LUNT:

"In 1833 there was a surplus revenue of many millions in the public treasury which by an act of legislation unparalled in the history of nations was distributed among the Northern States to be used for local public improvements."

PRESIDENT BUCHANAN, in his message to Congress, said:

"The South had not had her share of money from the treasury, and unjust discrimination had been made against her in coast defenses."

JOHN CODMAN ROPES, pp. 17 and 18:

"For many years before 1860 the Federal Government had all rifles and muskets manufactured near Troy, N. Y., to be deposited in Northern arsenals, so all the new guns were in possession of the North. After the attack by John Brown it was suggested that the South's quota of arms should be distributed, and Secretary Floyd then ordered the guns sent to the arsenals at Charleston, S. C., and the arsenals in North Carolina, Augusta, Ga., Mt. Vernon, Ala., and Baton Rouge, La. This was before Abraham Lincoln was nominated. This was done by an act of the Federal Government—not by any Southern statesman with any thought of war."

The unpreparedness for war, when war came, shows that the South did not even then receive anything like her just proportion.

SEE *Congressional Records:*

"It was a Pittsburg manufacturer that selfishly lobbied a bill through Congress for cannon to arm the unfurnished Southern forts. The bill was passed by the friends of the iron founders, without the knowledge of or solicitation of Secretary Floyd."

"Secretary Floyd simply obeyed Congress and ordered the arms sent but Secretary Holt, hearing of it, stopped the shipment, so the South never received the arms."

PERCY GREGG, p. 158, says:

"The Government was bound in honor to hand over to the seceding States their full share of armaments created at common expense."

IV.

The War Between the States Was Not Fought to Hold the Slaves

AUTHORITY:

A RESOLUTION was passed unanimously by Congress July 23, 1861:

"The war is waged by the Government of the United States, not in the spirit of conquest or subjugation, nor for the purpose of overthrowing or interfering with the rights or institutions of the states, but to defend and protect the Union."

ABRAHAM LINCOLN, in his Inaugural Address:

"I have no purpose directly or indirectly to interfere with the institution of slavery in the States where it exists. I believe I have no lawful right to do so, and I have no inclination to do so."

GEORGE LUNT'S *"Origin of the Late War,"* p. 432:

"A war simply for the abolition of slavery would not have enlisted a dozen regiments at the North."

Unanswerable arguments will be found in the facts that a slaveholder, General U. S. Grant, was placed in command of the Union Army, and General Robert E. Lee who had freed his

slaves put in command of the Confederate forces. Two hundred thousand slaveholders only were in the Southern Army
while three hundred and fifteten thousand slaveholders were in
the Northern Army.

GENERAL GRANT (Democratic Speaker's Handbook, p. 33), said:
> "Should I become convinced that the object of the Gov-
> ernment is to execute the wishes of the abolitionists, I
> pledge you my honor as a man and a soldier I would re-
> sign my commission and carry my sword to the other side."

SIMON CAMERON, Lincoln's Secretary of War, wrote to General
Butler in New Orleans:
> "President Lincoln desires the right to hold slaves to be
> fully recognized. The war is prosecuted for the Union
> hence no question concerning slavery will arise."

GOVERNOR WILLIAM SPRAGUE, Rhode Island's war Governor,
said:
> "We had to take a lot of abuse in return for an endorse-
> ment of Abraham Lincoln's Emancipation Proclamation.
> We were hissed in the streets and denounced as traitors."

JAMES FORD RHODES, Vol. IV, p. 73:
> "A large portion of our regular officers with many of the
> volunteers evidence far more solicitude to uphold slavery
> than to put down the rebellion."

PERCY GREGG:
> "To say that the South seceded and fought to hold her
> slaves is to accuse her of political imbecility."

CHANNING'S "Short History of the United States":
> "The Union Army showed the greatest sympathy with
> McClellan for the bold protest against emancipation. Five
> States, Indiana, Illinois, Ohio, Pennsylvania, and New York
> went against Lincoln on this account. While Lincoln felt
> he could free the slaves as a war measure, he knew the
> North would not approve of freeing them."

GEORGE LUNT, "Origin of the Late War":
> "Had not the Constitution provided for representation
> and taxation based on slave labor, and for the restoration
> of the fugitive slave there would have been no war—slavery
> was only an incident out of which grew questions regard-
> ing State rights and rights of Territories seeking to become
> States. But whether slavery was here rightfully or wrong-

fully it was here under the protection of the law and not
subject to be taken away by violence or any insidious device
of abstraction.''

GEORGE LUNT again says, p. 10 (Introduction):

"In presenting the causes which led to the war, it will be
seen that slavery, though an occasion was not in reality the
cause of the war.''

GEORGE LUNT, p. XII, (Introduction):

"Disregard of the rights of the South led to an unnatural
war, and the policy wrought an irreparable injury, if not
absolute ruin of the unhappy race they professed to love.''

GEORGE LUNT, p. XI, (Introduction):

"Anti-slavery was of no serious consequence until politicians seized upon it as an instrument of agitation—an
alleged diversity of interests between the sections involving
political power.''

CHASE, then Secretary of War under Lincoln, said:

"*Not war upon slavery within those limits,* but fixed opposition to its extension beyond them. Mr. Lincoln was the
candidate of the people not for abolition but as opposed to
the extension of slavery.''

V.

Slaves Were Not Ill-Treated in the South. The North Was Largely Responsible for Their Presence in the South.

AUTHORITY:

The servants were very happy in their life upon the old planta-
tions. WILLIAM MAKEPEACE THACKERAY, on a lecture tour in
America, visited a Southern plantation. In *"Roundabout
Papers"* he gives this impression of the slaves:

"How they sang! How they danced! How they laughed!
How they shouted! How they bowed and scraped and com-
plimented! So free, so happy! I saw them dressed on Sunday in their Sunday best—far better dressed than our
English tenants of the working class are in their holiday
attire. To me, it is the dearest institution I have ever seen
and these slaves seem far better off than any tenants I have
seen under any other tenantry system.''

MAJOR GENERAL QUITMAN of the United States Army thus de-
scribed life on the "Old Plantation" in 1822 while stationed in
Mississippi:

The mansions of the planters are thrown open to all
comers and goers free of charge. The owner of this planta-

tion is the widow of a Virginia gentleman of distinction, who was an officer in the last war with Great Britain.

"Her slaves are a happy, careless, unreflecting, good natured race. They are strongly attached to 'old massa,' and 'old missus'; but their devotion to 'young massa' and 'young missus' amounts to enthusiasm. While in a way these slaves appear to be free, they are very obedient and polite and they do their work well.

"These 'niggers,' as you call them, are the happiest people I have ever seen. They are oily, sleek, bountifully fed, well clothed and well taken care of. One hears them at all times whistling and singing cheerily at their work. . . . . . .

"But a negro will sleep—sleep at his work, sleep on his carriage box, sleep standing up, sleep bare-headed in the sun, and sleep sitting on a high rail fence. Yet, compared with the ague-smitten and suffering settlers in Ohio, or the sickly, half-starved operatives in the factories and mines of the North and the Northeast, these Southern slaves are indeed to be envied. They are treated with such great humanity and kindness."

CHAS. E. STOWE, the son of Harriet Beecher Stowe, in speaking at a negro college, said:

"If you ask me if the slaves were better off under the institution of slavery than they are under freedom, I must in candor answer that some were—they were not fit for freedom."

Again, he said:

"If slavery was an unutterably evil institution how can you account for the faithfulness of the negroes on the plantations when the men were at the front, and no act of violence known among them?"

AN EMINENT PENNSYLVANIA LAWYER said:

"An institution that could produce the Christian fidelity of 'Uncle Tom,' the faithful tenderness of 'Aunt Chloe,' and the patience and love of 'Eva's Mammy' must be indeed a great one!"

AMERICAN AUTHORS, p. 492:

"Slavery transformed the savage negro into a civilized man; it taught him to work, and showed him what could be accomplished by the labor of his hands; and then it left him as a free man with almost a monopoly of the field in which he had been employed as a slave. In 1865 no other body of negroes in the world occupied as advantageous a position economically as those in the Southern States."

"After 100 years of Southern civilization, the North voted

him the equal of the white man socially and politically—a marvelous tribute to the civilization of the Old South.''

If African slavery was a sin, the Spaniards and English were the sinners. It is true the slave trade in the United States was begun by Massachusetts, and in the main carried on by her, not as a private enterprise, but by the authority of the Plymouth Rock Colony. (*Colonial Entry Book*, Vol. IV., p. 724) .

The statute of establishing perpetual slavery was adopted by Massachusetts, December, 1641. (Massachusetts *Historical Collections*, VIII., p. 231).

The slave ship *Desire* sailed from Marblehead, Mass., and was the first to sail from any English colony in America to capture Africans.

The first State to legislate in favor of the slave trade was Massachusetts.

The first State to urge a fugitive slave law was Massachusetts. (Moore's *History of Slavery*).

The last State to legislate against the slave trade was Massachusetts. The British Encyclopedia says New Jersey.

The last slave ship to sail from the United States was the *Nightingale* from Massachusetts in 1861. She secured a cargo of 900 Africans, and was captured by the *Saratoga* under Captain Guthrie, April 21, 1861, after Fort Sumter had been fired on. There is no record that any punishment followed this violation of the law.

''The Cradle of Liberty,'' Fanueil Hall, in Boston, was built by Peter Faneuil, its owner, from slave trade money.

Girard College, in Philadelphia, was built by Stephen Girard with money made by African slaves on a Louisiana plantation.

The slaveholder has been accused of cruelty in separating mother and child on the slave block. The selling of slaves in the South did not separate mother and child as often or with such cruelty as did the slave traffic in Africa—as did the hiding of the fugitive slave from their owners—as did the ''Exodus Order'' in Reconstruction days.

White slavery in the North today is responsible for far more evils than ever came from the institution of slavery in the South.

The Southern planter has been accused of cruelty to his slaves —no cruelty on the part of any overseer can compare to that of the middle passage on the slave ships, where, on that long voyage, they were huddled as standing cattle and suffered from hunger and thirst so that they died by the hundreds, or cast themselves overboard.

Let it be remembered that no Southern man ever owned a slave ship. No Southern man ever commanded a slave ship. No Southern man ever went to Africa for slaves.

General Lee said, "There was no doubt that the blacks were immeasurably better off here than they were in Africa—morally, physically and socially." He thought the freeing of them should be left in God's hands and not be settled by tempestuous controversy.

The South has been vilified for not educating the negro in the days of slavery.

The South was giving to the negro the best possible education —that education that fitted him for the workshop, the field, the church, the kitchen, the nursery, the home. This was an education that taught the negro self-control, obedience and perseverance—yes, taught him to realize his weaknesses and how to grow stronger for the battle of life. The institution of slavery as it was in the South, so far from degrading the negro, was fast elevating him above his nature and his race.

No higher compliment was ever paid the institution of slavery than that by the North, which was willing to make the negro its social and political equal after one hundred years of civilization under Southern Christianizing influence. Never has it been recorded in history such rapid civilization from savagery to Christian citizenship.

The black man ought to thank the institution of slavery—the easiest road that any slave people have ever passed from savagery to civilization with the kindest and most humane masters. Hundreds of thousands of the slaves in 1865 were professing Christians and many were partaking of the communion in the church of their masters.—*"Civilization of the Old South,"* Historian-General, U. D. C., Dallas, Texas.

Coercion Was Not Constitutional

AUTHORITY:

WILLIAM SEWARD to *London Times* Correspondent, Mr. Russell, April 4, 1861:

"It would be contrary to the spirit of the American Government to use force to subjugate the South."

MR. SEWARD to Charles Francis Adams, Sr., Minister to England, April 10, 1861:

"Only a despotic and imperial government car ›oerce seceding States."

EDWARD EVERETT:

"To try to hold fifteen States to the Union is preposterous."

PRESIDENT JAMES BUCHANAN to Edwin M. Stanton, Secretary of War:

"There is no power under the Constitution to coerce a seceding State."

THE NEW YORK HERALD:

"The day before Fort Sumter was surrendered two-thirds of the newspapers in the North opposed coercion in any shape or form, and sympathized with the South. Three-fifths of the entire American people sympathized with the South. Over 200,000 voters opposed coercion and believed the South had a right to secede."

"*The Journal of Commerce* fought coercion until the United States mail refused to carry its papers in 1861."

CHARLES SUMNER said:

."Nothing can possibly be so horrible, so wicked or so foolish as a war against the South."

JAMES S. THAYER, of New York, on January 21, 1861, said:

"If the incoming Administration shall attempt to carry out a line of policy which has been foreshadowed, and construct a-scaffold for coercion—another name for execution—we will reverse the order of the French Revolution and save the blood of the people by making those who would inaugurate a 'Reign of Terror' the first victim of a national guillotine." (Enthusiastic applause).

CHARLES BEECHER STOWE said:

"Many patriotic men of the South who cared little or nothing about slavery were stirred with the deepest indignation at the suggestion of the National government subduing a sovereign State by force of arms, and said that a Union that could only be held together by bayonets had better be dissolved; and for the principle of State rights and State sovereignty the Southern men fought with a holy ardor and self-denying patriotism that have covered even defeat with imperishable glory."

JAMES BUCHANAN'S MESSAGE, December 3, 1860:

"Congress may possess many means of preserving the Union by conciliation, but the sword was not placed in its hand to preserve it by force."

LINCOLN, when asked how he could advocate coercion, replied:

"What is to become of my revenue in New York if there is a ten per cent. tariff at Charleston?"

GEORGE LUNT:

"The majority in the North believed that Lincoln had no right to coerce the States."

IN THE AMERICAN STATESMEN SERIES, Morse in Vol. II., "*Life of Abraham Lincoln*," says:

"History is crowded with tales of despots, but of no despot who thought or decided with the taciturn independence which marked this president of the Free American Republic in regard to coercing seceding States."

IN THE PLATFORM of the Republican Party is found this statement:

"We denounce the lawless invasion by armed force of the soil of any State or Territory, *no matter what pretext*, as among the gravest crimes."

SENATOR TRUMBULL, of Illinois, the special expositor of Mr. Lincoln's views, said in a speech in the Senate:

"Congress adjourned without taking action on coercion, showing, of course, the prevalent opinion on the Constitutional question." (Carpenter's "*Logic of History*," p. 50).

HORACE GREELEY, "*American Conflict*," p. 513:

"There was not a moment when a large portion of the Northern Democracy were not hostile to any form or shade of coercion. Many openly condemned and stigmatized a war on the South as *atrocious, unjustifiable,* and *aggressive."*

Ex-Governor Reynolds, Illinois, December 28, 1860

"I am heart and soul with the South. She is right in principle from the Constitution."

VII.

The Federal Government Was Responsible for the Andersonville Horrors

AUTHORITY:

Charles A. Dana, Assistant Secretary of War, said:

"We think after the testimony given that the Confederate authorities and especially Mr. Davis ought not to be held responsible for the terrible privations, suffering, and injuries which our men had to endure while kept in Confederate Military Prisons, the fact is unquestionable that while Confederates desired to exchange prisoners, to send our men home, and to get back their own men, General Grant steadily and strenuously resisted such an exchange."—*New York Sun.*

General Butler said:

"The reason for this was that the exchange of prisoners would strengthen Lee's army and greatly prolong the war."

General Grant said:

"Not to take any steps by which an able-bodied man should be exchanged until orders were received from him."

Secretary of War Edwin M. Stanton's statistics testify that while there were fifty thousand more of prisoners in Southern prisons than in Northern, the mortality among Southern men in Northern prisons was far greater.

General Grant, again, said:

If we hold these men caught they are no more than dead men. If we liberate them we will have to fight on until the whole South is exterminated."

This agrees with General Lee's *testimony* (*Official Records War of the Rebellion*):

"I offered General Grant to send into his lines all of the

prisoners within my Department provided he would return man for man. When I notified the Confederate authorities of my proposition, I was told if accepted they would gladly place at my disposal every man in our Southern prisons. I also made this offer to the Committee of the United States Sanitary Commission—but my propositions were not accepted.''

There was never any trouble about lack of provisions at Andersonville, as has been so often stated. There was an abundant supply of the rations that the soldiers and prisoners needed, but the trouble came because of the over-crowded condition of the stockade. It was made for 10,000 and in four months 29,000 were sent.

There were 6,000 sick in the hospitals at one time and no medicine—the first time in the history of wars when medicine was made contraband of war.

MEDICINE CONTRABAND OF WAR. (See Dr. Gardner's testimony).

"The United States government early declared by proclamation or order all medicines, surgical instruments and appliances contraband of war, and they were so regarded to the end of the struggle.

"The ill temper and inhumanity of the time in the North extended even to the medical profession, as evidenced at the convention of the American Medical Association, held in Chicago, in 1863, when Dr. Gardner, of New York, introduced preamble and resolutions petitioning the Northern government to repeal the orders declaring medical and surgical appliances contraband of war; arguing that such cruelty rebounded on their own soldiers, many of whom, as prisoners in the hands of the Confederates, shared the suffering resulting from such a policy, while the act itself was worthy the dark ages of the world's history. It is lamentable to have to record that this learned and powerful association of the medical men then limited to the North, forgetful of the noble and unselfish teachings of the healing art, in their senseless passion hissed their benevolent brother from the hall.

"The Northern government also resisted all efforts to effect a satisfactory agreement regarding the exchange of prisoners; only closing its eyes and pretending not to be aware of the informal agreements of opposing generals in the field as to the exchange of prisoners in their hands, respectively, till July 22, 1862, when a general cartel was agreed upon by the two governments, but which was never

carried out satisfactorily, and, in 1864, was practically suspended altogether; so that even the great prisons became inadequate for the increased demands upon them. Had there
been satisfactory agreement and good faith in carrying out
the cartels, Andersonville would not have been established,
and there would have been avoided that distressing calamity; and the effort which grew out of it to blacken the character of President Davis, and the persecution of Major
Henry Wirz, and his cruel execution by hanging. Justice
has never been done that noble heroism which resisted and
spurned the base and formidable bribe of life and liberty,
and held fast to the truth. The Southern people should ever
hold his memory dear.''

There were not enough vessels in which the food could be
properly prepared and served, and the Confederate authorities
were powerless, for they could not obtain these vessels to supply
the need.

GENERAL BUTLER says on pp. 593, 594 of his book:

, If the Confederates should be released and should join
Lee they would probably bring failure to General Grant's
operations. If on the other hand, they were released and
should join Sherman they would turn the scales against
him.''

In other words it was safer to allow the soldiers to remain
in Confederate pens, no matter how great their suffering, than
to liberate those Confederates.

GEORGE SHEA in a letter to the *New York Tribune,* January 24,
1876, said:

''Mr. Horace Greeley received a letter from Mrs. Jefferson
Davis June 22, 1865, imploring him to bring about a speedy
trial of her husband upon the charge of assassination of
President Lincoln, and the supposed cruelties at Andersonville Prison.''

A public trial was prayed in order that the accusations might
be publicly met, and her husband speedily vindicated.

CHARLES A. DANA, Assistant Secretary of War, said in the *New
York Sun:*

Mr. Greeley came to my residence and placed the letter in
my hands, saying he personally did not believe the charge
of complicity in the assassination of Lincoln to be true, and
that Mr. Davis could be released.

"We called Mr. Greeley's attention to the charge against Mr. Davis of cruel treatment of Union soldiers at Andersonville.

"There was a general opinion among the gentlemen of the Republican party that Mr. Davis *did not by thought* or *act participate in a conspiracy against Mr. Lincoln*, and none were more emphatic than Mr. Thaddeus Stevens.

"The only remaining charge, then, was the cruel treatment of the Andersonville prisoners, so at the suggestion of Mr. Greeley, Mr. Wilson and Mr. Stevens, I went to Canada to examine the official archives of the Confederate States. From these documents, not meant for public eyes, but used in secret session, it was evident that Mr. Davis *was not guilty of that charge.* I reported this at once to Mr. Greeley.

On November 9, 1866, this notice, evidently written by him, appeared in *The Tribune:*

" 'Eighteen months have nearly elapsed since Jefferson Davis was made a State prisoner. He has been publicly charged with conspiracy to assassinate President Lincoln and $100,000 offered for his capture upon this charge. The capture was made, and the money paid, yet no attempt has been made by the government to procure an indictment on this charge. He has been charged with the virtual murder of Union soldiers while prisoners of war at Andersonville— but no official attempt has been made to indict him on this charge.

" '*A great government may deal sternly with offenders, but not meanly; it cannot afford to seem unwilling to repair an obvious wrong.*' '

CHAS. A. DANA, *New York Sun:*

"It was not Jefferson Davis or any subordinate or associate of his who should now be condemned for the horrors of Andersonville. We were responsible ourselves for the continued detention of our captives in misery, starvation and sickness in the South."

MR. DANA again says:

"Of the charge of cruelty to our prisoners so often brought against Mr. Davis, and reiterated by Mr. Blaine in his speech in the United States Senate, we think Mr. Davis must be held altogether acquitted."

DR. KERR, in an address in New Orleans, said:

"Thirteen of the acts of cruelty which convicted Captain Wirz were committed when he was sick in bed and some one else was in charge of the prisoners."

DR. E. A. FLEWELLEN, who was sent *by the Federal authorities* to inspect the Andersonville prison told Dr. Kerr, the Confederate surgeon in charge, that he was

> "Most pleasantly impressed with Captain Wirz as an officer, and so reported to the Federal authorities, but as I heard nothing from this report supposed it suffered the fate of other papers belonging to the office of the surgeon general."

He further said:

> "I was present at Wirz's trial and can affirm every statement you made in your address at New Orleans as to the unfairness of the proceedings, and shall never cease to have a contempt for the president and judge advocate of that court martial for their efforts to intimidate the witnesses and pervert the truth, and for the disrespect shown to Wirz's only attorney, Louis Schade."

Dr. Kerr says that Wirz was called hard-hearted and cruel, but he has seen the tears streaming down his face when in the hospitals watching the sufferings of those men. Not a man ever died that he did not see that his grave was distinctly marked so that his mother could come and claim that body.

If the soldiers hated Wirz, as was said in the trial, why did they not kill him, for they had ample opportunity, as he never went armed. He did not even carry a pocket knife. He once laughingly said to Dr. Kerr that he had an old rusty pistol, but it would not shoot.

Six paroled prisoners drew up some resolutions when they returned from Washington, exonerating the Confederate authorities of all blame connected with the horrors of Andersonville prison life, and testifying to the fact that the insults received at Secretary Stanton's hands were far harder to bear than anything they ever had suffered at Andersonville. . See Page's "*True History of Andersonville*").

James Madison Page, a prisoner at Andersonville, wrote a book exonerating Captain Wirz and the Confederate authorities. Some of the prisoners sent a letter with a watch which they presented to Captain Wirz as a token of their appreciation of his kind treatment of them. Mrs. Perrin, Wirz's daughter, has many testimonials of this kind.

There was never any trouble about lack of provisions at An-

dersonville, as has been so often stated. There was an abundant supply of the rations that the soldiers and prisoners needed,
but the trouble came because of the over-crowded condition of
the stockade.

There were many bad men among the prisoners called "bounty
jumpers," and they were killed by their own men, yet Captain
Wirz was accused of their murder. Dr. Kerr said when Captain
Wirz paroled those six prisoners to send them North to plead
for an exchange, he turned to him and said, "I wish I could
parole the last one of them." At the surrender he went to
Macon, relying on the honor of General Wilson's parole. Im-
agine his surprise when he was arrested. He was taken to trial,
condemned upon suborned testimony and hanged November 6,
1865. That was the foulest blot in American history, and Mrs.
Surratt's death for complicity with John Wilkes Booth may be
placed beside it.

If any one questions the truth of these facts, they can be
found verified in the volumes called the "*War of the Rebellion,*"
in the Congressional Library in Washington, D. C., put there by
the United States authorities.—Series 2, Vols. IV., V., and VIII.,
and Series 3, Vol. V., and Page's "*True Story of Andersonville
Prison.*"

HERMAN A. BRAUM, of Milwaukee, Wis., who was also a prisoner
at Andersonville, after paying a tribute to Captain Wirz and
exonerating the Confederate authorities, says:

> "I believe that there is nothing so well calculated to
> strengthen the faith in popular government as the example
> given by the Confederacy during the war, its justice, hu-
> manity and power. On this rests the historic fame of Jef-
> ferson Davis.
> "In vain did the Confederate government urge an ex-
> change of prisoners. Union generals and Union civilians
> agreed that it would never do to let these Rebs go back to
> the firing line."

General Ben F. Butler says (see "*Butler's Book,*" pp. 592-
3-4), that General U. S. Grant and he held a conference at
Fortress Monroe, April, 1864, on this very matter.

Major Robert Ould, Confederate States Commissioner of Exchange, was then at the mouth of James River on the C. S.
Steamer, *Roanoke,* for the purpose of arranging for the delivery
and exchange of prisoners.

At the conference between Generals Grant and Butler it was finally decided that they would agree to accept such Union captives as the Confederates might see fit to surrender, *but that no Confederate prisoners would be delivered in return!*

GENERAL BUTLER was a man who, in many respects, was brutally frank and fearless, and he put on record the reason why General Grant and himself refused the offer to exchange:

"Many a tribute has been paid to the soldier of the South by those for whom he fought, by those of the same blood and faith, by those who gloried in his splendid courage and pitied his terrible sufferings; but the highest compliment that ever was paid to the tattered and half-starved wearer of the gray was that of the Commander-in-chief of the Union armies who, *in a council of war,* took the ground that *the Confederate prisoner was* too *dangerous to be exchanged.*"

VIII.

The Republican Party That Elected Abraham Lincoln Was Not Friendly to the South

AUTHORITY

WENDELL PHILLIPS:

"The Republican party is in no sense a National party; it is a party pledged to work for the downfall of Democracy, the downfall of the Union, and the destruction of the United States Constitution. The religious creed of the party was hate of Democracy, hate of the Union, hate of the Constitution, and hate of the Southern people."

Again, he says:

"The Republican party is the first sectional party ever organized in this country. It does not know its own face and calls itself National, but it is not National, it is sectional. It is the party of the North pledged against the South. It was organized with hatred of the Constitution.

"The Republican party that elected Abraham Lincoln is pledged to the downfall of the Union and the destruction of the United States Constitution.

"William Lloyd Garrison believed in the Constitutional right to hold slaves, and said the Union must be dissolved to free them.

"He believed in the Constitutional right of secession, so was willing to publicly burn the Constitution to destroy that right and called it 'a compact with death and a league with hell.' "

CHARLES BEECHER STOWE said:

"The party that elected Abraham Lincoln was a party avowedly hostile to the institution of slavery."

Had they not heard him say in his address at Cooper Institute that:

"The anti-slavery sentiment had already caused more than a million votes. which could only be seen by Southern States to mean a danger and menace. Consequently when they drew the sword to defend the doctrine of States rights and the institution of slavery, they certainly had on their side the Constitution and the laws of the land, for the National Constitution justified the doctrine of State rights."

R. G. HORTON, in his "A Youth's History of the Civil War," (Pubs., Van Evrie & Horton Co., N. Y., 1867, p. IV), says:

"Mr. Lincoln assumed the dictatorship, overthrew the government as it was formed by issuing a military edict or decree which changed the fundamental law of the land, and declared that he would maintain this by all the military and naval power of the United States."

GEORGE LUNT says, on page 369:

"Mr. Lincoln, finding a geographical party in the process of formation, allowed himself to be placed at its head, and encouraged its action by that sectional declaration, 'I believe this government cannot permanently endure half slave and half free.' That expression gave hope to the abolitionists, and defeated Stephen Douglas."

BENJAMIN F. WADE, a Senator from Ohio in 1860, and he did not love the South, said:

"I do not blame the people of the South for seceding for the men of that party about to take the reins of government in their hands are her mortal foes, and stand ready to trample her institutions under feet."

JUDGE WILLIAM DUER, of Oswego, New York, August 6, 1860, said:

"The Republican party is a conspiracy under the form, but in violation of the spirit of the Constitution of the United States to exclude the citizens of slaveholding States from all sharing in the government of the country, and to compel them to adapt their institutions to the opinions of the citizens of the free States."

GEORGE LUNT says, again, on p. 359:

> "The nomination of Mr. Lincoln was purely accidental, and that he was a sectional candidate upon merely sectional grounds none can deny and for the first time in the history of the republic, a candidate was thus presented for the suffrages of its citizens."

MR. RAYMOND, in the *New York Times*, says:

> "His election was more by shouts and applause which dominated the convention than from any direct labors of any of the delegates."—*Boston Courier*, May 26, 1860.

GEORGE LUNT:

> Judge Jessup's amendment openly professed the party to be sectional."

STEPHEN DOUGLAS, in his letter to Mr. Hayes, December 27, 1860, said: .

> "Many Republicans desire a dissolution of the Union and *urge war* as a means of accomplishing dissolution."

Again Mr. Douglas, February 2, 1861, said:

> "The leaders of the Republican party are striving to break up the Union under pretense of unbounded devotion to it. Hostility to slavery on the part of the disunionists is stronger than fidelity to the Constitution."

HORTON again says:

> "I shall stress that this war was not waged by the North to preserve the Union, or to maintain Republican institutions, but to destroy both.
> "It will be seen that the war changed the entire character and system of our government, overthrew the rights of States, and forced amendments against the action of the people."

R. G. HORTON, again, said, p. 51 of his *"Youth's History of the Civil War"*:

> "At the very time the abolitionists were preaching a mad crusade against the Union, and educating a generation to hate the government of our fathers, Southern men, the great leaders of the South, were begging and imploring that the Union might be preserved."

The Cincinnati Enquirer, January 15, 1881, said:

> "Republican hate has blasted the fair heritage of our fathers. The prediction made two years before Daniel

Webster's death has literally come true. He said: 'If these fanatics (abolitionists) ever get the power in their own hands they will override the Constitution, set the Supreme Court at defiance, change and make laws to suit themselves, lay violent hands on them who differ in opinion, or who dare question their fidelity, and finally deluge the country with blood.''

IX.

The South Desired Peace and Made Every Effort to Obtain It

AUTHORITY:

THE MISSISSIPPI CONVENTION sent a commissioner to Maryland and when asked what was the intention of the Southern States by secession, (Shaffner's "*Secession War,*" London, 1862), he replied:

"Secession is not intended to break up the present government, but to perpetuate it. Our plan is to withdraw from the Union in order to allow amendments to the Constitution to be made, guaranteeing our just rights. If the Northern States will not make these amendments—then we must secure them ourselves by a government of our own."

LORD CHARNWOOD's "*Life of Lincoln*":

"This madness appeared when the Congress met in December, 1860. In order to allay the apprehensions of the Southern people regarding the purposes of the party just ready to come into power, the Southern members offered resolution after resolution looking to tranquility. These resolutions were all rejected by the House of Representatives.

"Then was offered in the Senate the celebrated 'Crittenden Compromise,' yielding all that the North demanded in regard to exclusion of slavery from the Territories, but insisting that the Constitution be respected as to fugitive slaves, and that the Constitution be maintained and its provision be kept as adjudicated by the Supreme Court of the land. The South made no new request; it went not outside of the Constitution. It rested its case on the Constitution and on its interpretation by the highest court of the land. It was strictly loyal to the Constitution.

Why was the Crittenden Compromise rejected? Because Mr. Lincoln willed it. He wrote letters to his party leaders to defeat it. He said 'he had no compromises to make with the South.' The idea was that he had triumphed and that triumph meant no surrender in any respect of the new policies.

"It was a tragic day when the Crittenden Compromise was defeated. Not a single Republican voted for it.

The Crittenden Resolutions were a most generous proposition from the South to allow out of the 1,200,000 square miles of territory acquired by conquest and purchase, 900,000 square miles for free territory and the remaining 300,000 square miles to be free or slave as each new State formed might choose, and this, too, when Southern prowess had largely gained the territory. These resolutions in the interest of peace were offered by Northern and Southern Democrats. Lincoln notified all Republican States through Senators Harlan and Zach Chandler to vote against these resolutions. Had he not done this they would have passed. Unjust as they were to the South, the South would have accepted them, and Thurlow Weed and Seward would have seen that they were passed by the North. It was Lincoln's fault they were rejected. George Lunt said Lincoln later acknowledged that he regretted this.

Again Lord Charnwood said:

"Senator Chandler, of Michigan, had telegraphed to the Governor of Michigan to send delegates to the Péace Congress, 'but to send stiff-necked men or none—for without a little blood letting the Union will not be worth saving.'"

GEORGE LUNT, p. 423, says:

"The propositions of the Peace Conference evidently formed a sound basis for settlement of the controversy. These resolutions were introduced by Mr. Crittenden, of Kentucky, and had they been adopted, they would have saved the country from its coming trials. On the committee of thirteen reporting these resolutions were Jefferson Davis, of Mississippi; Mr. Hunter, of Virginia; Robert Toombs, of Georgia; five from slave States—eight from free States. General Toombs' reported to his constituents in Georgia that the Black Republican solidly voted against the resolutions. Mr. Douglas, in the Senate, said: 'Every member from the South including *Messrs. Davis and Toombs,* from the Cotton States, expressed a willingness to accept the resolutions as a final settlement of the controversy. Hence the responsibility of our disagreement, and the only difficulty in the way of an amicable adjustment is with the Republican party." (See *Congressional Globe,* Appendix 1800-61, p. 41).

"Mr. Toombs, in the Senate, said there were some conditions he would prefer, but for the sake of peace—permanent peace—he would accept them."

Mr. Pugh, of Ohio, said he had heard the senator from Mississippi (afterwards President Davis) before leaving the Senate Chamber say he would accept it to maintain the Union. There is no doubt but that a two-thirds vote would have saved the Union."

When it came to a final vote *every Republican voted against them except Mr. Seward who refused* to vote at all. The resolutions were lost by a vote of 20 to 19. How could peace have been brought about?

MR. DIXON, of Connecticut, in 1860, had the true idea. He said:

"The true way to restore harmony is by cheerfully and honestly assuring every section its Constitutional rights. No section professes to ask more; no section ought to offer less."

MR. BROWN, a personal friend and colleague of Jefferson Davis, of Mississippi, replied:

"If that same spirit could prevail which actuates the senator from Connecticut, who has just taken his seat, a different state of things might be produced in twenty days."

THE REJECTION of the Crittenden Resolutions created a crisis:

"The Southern leaders then called a conference. What was to be done? All their proposals of compromise, looking to peace, tranquility, security within the Union, had failed. They asked each other: 'What is the purpose of this anti-South party? What means the rejection of our compromises? Why did Mr. Lincoln discountenance any compromise? What means this secession from the Constitution? This refusal to abide by the decisions of the United States Supreme Court? What means Mr. Lincoln's attitude in opposing the Crittenden Compromise?'

"Despairing of their rights within the Union, the Southern leaders advised the Southern States to throw themselves back on their reserved rights and withdraw from the Union. But it was too late. It could have been done in 1850, but not in 1861. From 1850 to 1860 the North had educated the people of the North out of the Jefferson theory of State rights."—*George Lunt.*

SECOND PEACE CONGRESS, Ex-President John Tyler, President, Washington, D. C.:

"Virginia did not act at the time with the Southern

States that organized the Confederacy, but called a 'Peace Conference.' Twenty-one States responded to the call. The venerable John--Tyler, ex-President of the United States, was chosen president. They met in Washington on February 4, 1861. But Salmon P. Chase, to be the Secretary of the Treasury under the new administration, was there as the representative of Mr. Lincoln and the new victorious party... His speech destroyed all hope of any reconciliation. He refused all compromises, and said Northern States would never fulfill that part of the Constitution in regard to fugitive slaves, and that the decision of the Supreme Court would not be abided. The failure of this conference was a great disappointment, especially to Virginia. Mr. Lincoln took the same stand as he did regarding the Crittenden. Compromise."—Lord Charnwood's "*Life of Lincoln.*"

JUDGE SALMON P. CHASE in Peace Congress:

"I must tell you further that under no inducements whatever will we consent to surrender a principle which we believe to be sound, and so important as that of restricting slavery within State limits."

And again he said:

"The people of the free States who believe that slavery is wrong cannot and will not aid in returning runaway slaves and the law becomes a dead letter."

Now, this was in defiance of the decision of the Supreme Court in the Dred Scott case.

SECRETARY CHASE announced that:

"The Republican party would concede nothing in regard to slave extension in the Territories, and the Northern States would never fulfill their Constitutional obligations." (There was nothing to do but to adjourn).

THE third attempt was when the Peace Commissioners were sent from the Confederate government with this message:

"The undersigned are instructed to make to the Government of the United States overtures for the opening of negotiations, assuring the Government of the United States that the President, Congress, and people of the Confederate States earnestly desire *a peaceful solution of these great questions;* that it is neither their interest nor their wish to make any demand which is not founded in strictest justice, nor do any act to injure their late Confederates."

A peaceful spirit would have kept peace—who was responsible for the answer?

HAMPTON ROADS CONFERENCE the last:

"At Hampton Roads, Lincoln refused to accept any proposals except unconditional surrender. He promised clemency but refused to define it, except to say that he individually favored compensation for slave owners, and that he would execute the confiscation and other penal acts with the utmost liberality. He made it plain throughout that he was fighting for an idea, and that it was useless to talk of compromise until that idea was triumphant. We are aware, of course, of that long-exploded myth telling how he offered Stephens a sheet of paper with 'Union' written on it, and told the Confederate statesman to fill up the rest of the paper to suit himself. 'He offered us nothing but unconditional submission,' says Stephens on his return, and he called the conference, therefore, fruitless and inadequate."
—*New York Times.*

Abraham Lincoln testifies the same. See Lincoln's *Message* to *House,* Feb. 10, 1865; "*War of the Rebellion,*" Series 1, Vol. XLVI, p. 505; Lincoln's *Instructions to Seward,* Jan. 31, 1865; "*Life of Lincoln,*" Nicolay & Hay, Vol X.; Seward's *Letter to Charles Francis Adams; "War of Rebellion,*" Series III, Vol. IV., pp. 1163-1164.

X.

The Policy of the Northern Army Was to Destroy Property— That of the Southern Army to Protect It

AUTHORITY:

SHERIDAN'S OFFICIAL REPORT:

"I have burned two thousand barns filled with wheat and corn, all the mills in the whole country, destroyed all the factories of cloth, killed or driven off every animal, even the poultry that could contribute to human sustenance.

"Nothing should be left in the Shenandoah but eyes to lament the war."

SHERMAN'S *Memoirs:*

"It will not be necessary to sow salt on the site of Charleston after the Fifteenth Corps has done its work."

"One hundred million dollars of damage has been done

to Georgia; $20,000,000 inured to our benefit, the remainder simply waste and destruction."

"On General Howell Cobb's plantation I told my men to spare nothing."

"I'll not restrain the army lest its vigor and energy be impaired." (p. 185).

"In South Carolina I kindled my fire with an old mantel clock, and a piece of a handsome old bedstead." (p. 225).

"Orders to kill Jeff Davis and his Cabinet on the spot" were found on the person of Dahlgren in Richmond, Va.

Lord Palmerson in the British House of Commons took occasion to express deepest indignation at General Butler's infamous order No. 28 against the ladies of New Orleans.

GENERAL GRANT to Hunter in the Shenandoah Valley, Virginia:

"Nothing shall be left to invite the enemy to return."

'"City Point, July 14, 1864.

"'Major-General Halleck, Washington, D. C.

"'If the enemy has left Maryland, as I suppose he has, he should have upon his heels veterans, militiamen, men on horseback, and everything that can be got to follow to eat out Virginia clear and clean as they go, so that the crows flying over it will have to carry their provender with them.

"(Signed)   U. S. GRANT,

"'Lieutenant-General.'"

"'City Point, August 26, 1864.

"'Major-General Sheridan, Halltown, Va.:

"'Do all the damage to railroads and crops you can. Carry off stock of all descriptions and negroes, so as to prevent further planting. We want the Shenandoah Valley to remain a barren waste.

"'(Signed)   U. S. GRANT,

"'Lieutenant-General.'"

"'Headquarters Middle Military Division,

"'Harrisburg, Sept. 28, 1864, 10:30 p. m.

"'Brig.-Gen. W. Merritt, Commanding First Cavalry Division:

"'General: , The general commanding directed that you leave a small force to watch Swift Run and Brown Gap and with balance of your command and Custer's Division to swing around through or near Piedmont, extending toward and as near Staunton as possible. Destroy all mills, all grain, and all forage you can and drive off or kill all stock and otherwise carry out instructions of Lieutenant-General

Grant, an extract of which is sent you and which means 'leave a barren waste.'

" ' (Signed) JAMES W. FORSYTH,

" 'Lieut.-Col. and Chief of Staff to General Sheridan.' "

" 'Headquarters of the Army, Washington, D. C.,

" 'December 18, 1864.

" 'Major-General Sherman, Savannah:

" 'Should you capture Charleston, I hope that by some accident the place may be destroyed; and if a little salt should be sown upon the site, it may prevent the growth of future crops of nullification and secession.

" ' (Signed) W. H. HALLECK,

" ' Chief of Staff.' "

" 'Field Headquarters of the Military Division of
    the Mississippi, Savannah, December 24, 1864.

" 'Major-General W. H. Halleck, Chief of Staff, Washington, D. C.:

" 'I will bear in mind your hint as to Charleston, and I do not think 'salt' will be necessary. When I move, the Fifteenth Corps will be on the right of the right wing, and their postiion will bring them into Charleston first; and if you have watched the history of this corps, you will have remarked that it generally does its work pretty well.

" 'The truth is, the whole army is burning with an insatiable desire to wreak vengeance upon South Carolina. I almost tremble at her fate, but feel that she deserves all that seems in store for her. We must make old and young, rich and poor, feel the hard hand of war as well as their organized armies.

" ' (Signed) W. T. SHERMAN,

" ' Major-General.' "

"*The Story of a Great March,*" Brevet Major George W. Nichols, Aide-de-Camp to General Sherman:

"History will in vain be searched for a parallel to the scathing and destructive effect of the invasion of the Carolinas. Aside from the destruction of military things, there were destructions overwhelming, overleaping the present generation—even if peace speedily come, agriculture, commerce, cannot be revived in our day. Day by day our legions of armed men surged over the land, over a region of forty miles wide, burning everything we could not take away. On every side the head, center and rear of our columns might be traced by columns of smoke by day and the glare of flames by night. The burning hand of war pressed on these people, blasting, withering."

Major Nichols, *"The Story of a Great March*, November 15, 1864 (p. 38), Atlanta, Ga.:

"A grand and awful spectacle is presented to the beholders of this beautiful city now in flames. The Heaven is one expanse of lurid fire. The air is filled with flying, burning cinders. Buildings covering 200 acres are in ruins or flames."

"We are leaving Atlanta. Behind we leave a track of smoke and flame. Yesterday we saw in the distance a pillar of smoke; the bridges were all in flames. I heard a soldier say, 'I believe Sherman has set the very river on fire.' His comrades replied, 'If he has its all right.' The rebel inhabitants are in an agony. The soldiers are as hearty and jolly as men can be." (p. 37).

"The soldiers are hunting for concealed things and these searches are one of the pleasant excitements of our march." (p. 39).

Sherman's *Memoirs*, Vol. II, p. 287:

"In my official report of the conflagration of Columbia I distinctly charged it to General Wade Hampton, and now I confess I did it pointedly to shake the faith of his people in him."

Gregg's *History*, p. 375:

"The devastation of the Palatine hardly exceeded the desolation and misery wrought by the Republican invasion and conquest of the South. No conquered nation of modern days, not Poland under the heel of Nicholas, nor Spain or Russia under that of Napoleon, suffered from such individual and collective ruin or saw before so frightful a prospect as the States dragged by force in April, 1865."

CONTRAST:

President Davis:

"In regard to the enemy's crews and vessels you are to proceed with the justice and humanity which characterize our government and its citizens."

"General Lee, for fear his soldiers should pillage while foraging in Pennsylvania, had the roll call three times daily."

It is true General Early did burn Chambersburg, Pa., but it was only after a refusal by the people to pay the $100,000 demanded for General Hunter's destruction in the Shenandoah Valley.

When at York, Pa., he was urged to burn that place in retaliation. He said:

"We do not make war on women and children."

GENERAL JOHN B. GORDON to the women in York, Pa.:

"If the torch is applied to a single dwelling or an insult offered to a woman by a soldier in my command, point me the man and you shall have his life."

CHARLES FRANCIS ADAMS testified:

"I doubt if a hostile foe ever advanced in an enemy's country or fell back from it in retreat leaving behind it less cause for hate and bitterness than did the Army of Northern Virginia."

R. E. LEE, Commanding General, Chambersburg, Penn., June 21, 1863:

"The commanding general considers that no greater disgrace could befall the army, and through it our whole people, than the perpetuation of the barbarous outrages upon the unarmed and defenseless and the wanton destruction of private property that have marked the course of the enemy in our own country.

"Such proceedings not only degrade the perpetrators and all conected with them, but are subversive of the discipline and efficiency of the army and destructive of the ends of our present movement. It must be remembered that we make war only upon armed men, and that we cannot take vengeance for the wrongs our people have suffered without lowering ourselves in the eyes of all whose abhorrence has been excited by the atrocities of our enemies and offending against Him to whom vengeance belongeth, without whose favor and support our efforts all prove in vain. The commanding general, therefore, earnestly exhorts the troops to abstain, with most scrupulous care, from unnecessary or wanton injury to private property, and he enjoins upon all officers to arrest and bring to summary punishment all who shall in any way offend against the orders on this subject."

PRESIDENT DAVIS said to his soldiers:

"The rules taught at West Point were: 'Private property can be seized only by way of military necessity for the support or benefit of the army of the United States. All wanton violence, pillage or sacking, maiming or killing is prohibited under penalty of death or punishment adequate for the gravity of the offense.' "

WILLIAM M. MACY, Secretary of War, July 28, 1856:

"The wanton pillage or uncompensated appropriation of individual property by an army, even in possession of an enemy's country is against the usage of modern times."

XI.

The South Has Never Had Her Rightful Place In Literature

AUTHORITY:

HARRIET MARTINEAU said:

"For more than fifty years after the Revolution the best specimen of periodical literature that this country afforded was 'The Southern Review,' published at Charleston, S. C., by Bledsoe."

HAMILTON W. MABIE placed Poe, Timrod and Lanier as equal in poetic quality with Bryant, Whittier and Longfellow. He said:

"In the widening literary activity the South has borne a very notable part—indeed, it may be said that it has borne the chief part.' '

PANCOAST, of Philadelphia, says:

"The Southern story writers have done more than given us studies of new localities. We feel instinctively a different quality in their work. Contrasted with the New England writers we feel the richer coloring, the warmer blood, and the quicker pulses. When you read Hawthorne and then turn to 'Marse Chan' and 'Meh Lady' by Thomas Nelson Page, it is like passing from the world of thought to the world of action—from the analysis of life to true living. It is a world where the men are full of knightly deeds."

HAMILTON MABIE said:

"The genius of the Old South went into the management of public affairs and gave the country a group of statesmen that will not suffer by comparison with the foremost public men of any country."

Then again:

"The South of today has no explanations to make; her quota of writers of original gift and genuine art is perhaps more important than that furnished by any other section of our country. These writers exhibit certain qualities of the Southern temperament from which much may be expected in the literature of the future. Their work comes from the heart rather than from analytical faculties. It is made of flesh and blood, and it is therefore simple, tender, humorous and altogether human, and those qualities give assurance that it has long life before it.''—*The Outlook.*

What does JOHN FISKE, a great historian of this century say?

While unjust to the South in many things he realizes the part the South has played in the making of the Nation:

"Jefferson, Washington, Madison, Marshall and Alexander Hamilton are distinguished above all others and in an especial sense they deserve to be called the founders of the American Union.

"The Declaration of Independence ranks with the Magna Charta and the Bill of Rights as one of the three greatest of State papers.

"John Marshall, Chief Justice for thirty years, settled the relations of the Executive, Legislative, and Judicial branches of the government.

"James Madison, as a constructive thinker, did more than all others not only to create the Constitution, but to secure its ratification."

What section of the country ever produced greater orators than Henry Clay, John C. Calhoun, John Forsyth, Benjamin H. Hill, Robert Toombs, Howell Cobb, Alexander Stephens, Robert Y. Hayne, William H. Yancey and a host of others?

The greatest American dramatist was Augustin Daly, North Carolina.

IN "*The Outlook*" in 1899 appeared this article from the pen of Hamilton Mabie:

"The South never lacked institutions to keep alive the best traditions of scholarship—never lacked culture to keep in touch with the best of thought and art in the Old World and the New. A love of letters was really keener in the South than in New England, and there was a much larger group of highly educated men in the South than in New England—but ethics and religion made literature of secondary importance.

"The genius of the Old South went into the management of public affairs, but it gave the country a group of statesmen who would add dignity to the most illustrious periods of statesmenship—such men as Washington, Jefferson, Madison, and Marshall—they will not suffer by comparison with the foremost public men of the country."

Pancoast, of Philadelphia, says:

"Put the work of Cable by the side of Howell's and it is like the tropic warmth of the Gulf Stream after the chill of Northern waters.

"The themes of the Southern writers are fresh, new, inspiring and striking—they write about the things with which they are familiar."

Victor Hugo called Edgar Allan Poe "The Prince of American Literature."

The London Quarterly Review said, "He had an ear for rhythm unmatched in all the ages." And Richardson says: "He is one of the world's men of genius."

Coleridge said:

"Washington Allston of South Carolina was the first genius of the Western World."

Tennyson said:

"Bryant, Whittier and other New England writers are pigmies compared with Poe. He is the literary glory of America."

Paul Hamilton Hayne has been called the "Woodland Minstrel of America." His *"Daphels"* has been pronounced by Lewisohn as "the finest narrative poem ever written," and Tennyson called him "the finest sonnet writer in America."

Hamilton Mabie, in *"The Outlook,"* said:

"Timrod's *"Cotton Boll"* and Lanier's *"Sunrise"* have been called 'the most original achievements of American poetry.'"

Longfellow said:

"The time will surely come when Timrod's poems will be in every home of culture."

Yet after this high praise, Brander Matthews in his *American Literature*, gives Lanier and Timrod *three lines*, does not mention Hayne or Father Ryan, but gives Harriet Beecher Stowe's *Uncle Tom's Cabin* an entire page.

Abernathy, in his *American Literature* gives *eleven* pages to Daniel Webster and *three lines* to Clay and Calhoun. He gives Franklin more space than he gives to Washington, Jefferson, Madison, Monroe, Marshall, Patrick Henry, Henry Laurens, the Randolphs, the Pinckneys and other Southern statesmen combined.

The New International Encyclopedia gives as much space to John Brown—a traitor and murderer—as is given to Robert Toombs, William H. Yancey, Alexander Stephens and other statesmen of the South combined.

The Columbia Encyclopedia gives John Brown as much or more space than is given to Jefferson Davis, United States Secretary of War and President of the Confederate States.

XII.

The North Violated the Constitution, and Refused to Stand by the Decisions of the Supreme Court, and This Drove the South to Secession

1. *The Missouri Compromise, 1820. Slave territory restricted* and no Constitutional authority for it.
2. *The Tariff Acts* of 1828 and 1833. The Constitution says tariff must be uniform—one section must not be discriminated against in favor of another.
3. *Violation of the Fugitive Slave Law.* Article IV., Sec. II., Clause 3.
4. *Coercion* in 1861. Article IV., Sec. IV.
5. *Laws of Neutrality—Trent Affair.* Article VI., Clause 2— Violation of International Law.
6. *Writ of Habeas Corpus Suspended.* Article I., Sec. IX., Clause 2.
7. *War Was Declared Without the Consent of Congress, 1861.* Article I., Section VIII., Clauses 11, 12.
8. *Emancipation Proclamation.* Article IV., Section III., Clause 2.
9. *West Virginia Made a State.* Article IV., Section III.. Clause 1.
10. *The Hanging of Mrs. Surratt.* Amendments—Article V.
11. *The Execution of Henry Wirz.* Amendments—Article VI.
12. *The XIV. and XV. Amendments.* Article V.
13. *The Seizure Without Compensation of Property After Surrender. _Amendments*—Articles IV. and VI.
14. *Squatter Sovereignty.* It allowed a territorial government to exclude slavery.
15. *The Liberty of the Press Taken Away.* Amendments—Article I.

16. *The Freedom of Speech Denied. Vallandigham Imprisoned in Ohio.* Amendments—Article I.

17. *Blockading Ports of States that Were Held by the Federal
Government to Be still in the Union.*

MISSOURI COMPROMISE.

PERCY GREGG, the English historian, says:

> "Baffled, wearied and worn out, the South reluctantly
> submitted to the Missouri Compromise. This was no com-
> promise but the extortion by naked force at an enormous
> price for the allowance of a right *iniquitiously and uncon-
> stitutionally withheld.*"

GEORGE LUNT, of Boston, Massachusetts, in his *"Origin of the
Late War,"* says:

> "Missouri was as fairly entitled to admission into the
> Union as a slave State, if its inhabitants so willed it, as
> Louisiana had come in as a slave State in 1812 or Iowa as
> a free State in 1846. It was, nevertheless, a struggle on the
> part of the North to impose political restrictions upon that
> enlargement of political power which it is feared the South
> might gain by increasing the number of States allied to
> it in interest and sympathy. It was the earliest open dem-
> onstration of organized jealousy."

GEORGE LUNT gives some resolutions passed unanimously by
the House of Representatives:

> "That neither the Federal government nor non-slave-
> holding States have a Constitutional right to legislate upon
> or interfere with slavery in any of the States in the Union."
> (p. 432).

The South again felt that the Compromises of 1850 were unjust because the Missouri line was made when the North wished
it and was done away with, when the North wished it, and that
the North, to carry her point, was willing to destroy not only
the Constitution but the very Union itself.

Hear what JOSIAH QUINCY, the standard bearer of the Republican party (Political Textbook, p. 108; Letter to Mr. Car-
ruthers, Feb. 28, 1856; George Lunt, p. 261), said:

> "Reinstate in full force that barrier against the exten-
> sion of slavery called the Missouri Compromise. Make
> Kansas a free State even if it *dissolves the Union itself.*"

JUDGE STORY, of the Supreme Court, in speaking of the Fugitive Slave Law, (Peters *Reports,* Pregg vs. Pa., p. 611), said:

"It cannot be doubted that it constituted a fundamental article, (the right to own slaves) without the adoption of which the Union could not have been formed."

TARIFF ACTS.

The South maintained that the Tariff Acts of 1828 and 1833 were unconstitutional, since Congress had the power to levy taxes only for revenue and the taxes must be uniform. The act then passed was sectional, since by it the South, while she had only one-third of the votes, paid two-thirds of the custom duties, and as our government was a compact, the government could not be superior to the States—so Congress was over-stepping its powers, and she contended that a tax on one part of the country could not be laid to protect the industries of another part. (Constitution—Section VIII., Clause 1).

The South contended that the Tariff Acts of 1828, 1832, and 1833 were violations of the Compact or Constitution for "taxation was not uniform," and one section was discriminated against in favor of the other. The Cotton States particularly suffered by these traiff acts.

What had the North to say to this?

When THOMAS HART BENTON, of Missouri, in referring to the Tariff Acts, said:

"Under Federal legislation the exports of the South have been the basis of the Federal revenues—everything goes out and nothing is returned to them in the shape of government expenditures. The expenditures flow North. This is the reason why wealth disappears from the South and rises up in the North. No tariff has yet included Georgia, Virginia, or the two Carolinas, except to increase the burdens imposed upon them. The political economists of the North, Carey, Elliott, Kettel and others who have studied the source of National wealth in America, said, 'Mr. Benton is right in the explanation given of the sudden disappearance of wealth from the South.'"

And when the abolitionists tried to contend that slavery was the cause of this not the tariff, Prof. Elliott, a teacher of Science at Harvard, denied that it was *slavery that had impoverished the South,* and said *it was Federal legislation in regard* to *the Tariff Acts.*

BLEDSOE'S *"War Between the States,"* (p. 225), said:

"This legislation, so unjust to the South, left in the minds of the men of the South a deep and abiding sense of the injustice of Northern legislation."

Then the editor of *"Southern Wealth and Northern Profits,"* a Northern man, said:

"It is gross injustice, if not hypocrisy, to be always growing rich on the profits of slave labor; and at the same time to be eternally taunting and insulting the South on acconut of slavery. Though you bitterly denounce slavery as the 'sum of all villainies,' it is nevertheless the principal factor (by high tariff) of your Northern wealth, and you know it."

FUGITIVE SLAVE LAW.

The South claimed that their slaves were their property, bought from the Northern slave dealer with their money, and not only could be protected by the Constitution but, by a later guarantee which had been given by the Compromises of 1850, returned to them when they ran away.

What does the North say?

CHIEF JUSTICE STORY, of the United States Supreme Court, said:

"The master has the right to seize the runaway slave in any State of the Union."

ABRAHAM LINCOLN, in a speech at Peoria, Ill., in 1854, said:

"The slaveholder has a legal and moral right to his slaves."

See also Amendment IV. of the United States Constitution.

JUDGE BLACK, in his *"Essays,"* p. 153, says:

"That 'Higher Law' which gave the Federal government power to legislate against the Southern States in defiance of the Constitution would logically justify any executive outrage that might be desired for party purposes on the life, liberty and property of individuals."

The interference on the part of Northern politicians with the institution of slavery and the rights of the slaveholder to take his slaves where he pleased was illegal and unconstitutional.

This claim was supported by Congress when Benjamin Franklin and the Quakers urged the freedom of the slaves. The decision was that Congress had no right to interfere with the institution of slavery or the slaveholders. (See Congressional Records).

It was again supported by the decision in the Dred Scott case —that a slave being carried into a free State did not give him his freedom—only the slaveholder himself had the right to free his slave. ((See Decision of Supreme Court—Taney).

THE HOUSE OF REPRESENTATIVES had passed the following reso lutions:

> "That Congress has no authority to interfere in the emancipation of slaves or in the treatment of them within any of the States; it remaining with the several States alone to provide any regulations there which humanity and true policy may require."

Lincoln violated the Constitution when he called for the militia to coerce the States.

VIRGINIA'S reply was:

> "Virginians will never join you in your open and known violation of the Constitution nor unite with your forces in shedding the blood of Virginia's brethren for support of the Union. If Virginians must fight they prefer to espouse the cause of the Constitution, the backbone of the Union."

EMANCIPATION.

> "Emancipation is not within the scope of the Constitution, or in any degree at the disposition of the United States government, and can mean nothing else than revolution for which the abolitionists are striving. Revolution can only be justified by oppression and the power of oppression is not with the South."

A RESOLUTION was passed unanimously by Congress July 23, 1861:

> "The war is waged by the government of the United States, not in the spirit of conquest or subjugation, nor for the purpose of overthrowing or interfering with the rights or institutions of the States, but to defend and maintain the supremacy of the Constitution, and to preserve the Union with all the dignity, equality and rights of the several States unimpaired."

McClure, an ardent admirer of Abraham Lincoln, says:

"As the sworn executive of the Nation, it was his duty to obey the Constitution, in all its provisions, and he accepted that duty without reservations—yet in eighteen months he issued his Emancipation Proclamation."

James Ford Rhodes, of Massachusetts, Vol. IV, p. 213, says:

"There was, as every one knows, no authority for the proclamation in the letter of the Constitution, nor was there any statute that warranted it."

The Supreme Court of the United States in its ruling said:

"Any doctrine which leads to the suspension of any of the provisions of the Constitution during the exigencies of government leads directly to anarchy or despotism."

Chief Justice Chase said:

"Neither President, nor Congress, nor Courts possess any power not given by the Constitution."

Abraham Lincoln said:

"I have no Constitutional right to free your slaves and I have no desire to do so."

Horton, in his "Youth's History of the Civil War," p. 51, says:

"The great leaders of the South were begging and imploring that the Union should be preserved."

FREEDOM OF SPEECH.

As was the case of Vallandigham in Ohio men were thrown into prison for daring to say the South was right.

James Ford Rhodes, (Vol. III., p. 232), says:

"Mr. Lincoln stands responsible for the casting into prisons citizens of the United States on orders as arbitrary as the *Lettres De Cachet* of Louis XIV. of France, instead of their arrest as in Great Britain in her crisis on legal arrests"

George Bancroft, "*Life of Seward*," (Vol. II, p. 254), says:

"Some of the features of these arbitrary arrests bore a striking resemblance to the odious institution of the ancient regime of France—the Bastile and *Lettres De Cachet*."

WRIT OF HABEAS CORPUS SUSPENDED.

ABRAHAM LINCOLN, Albany, N. Y.:

"The suspension of the habeas corpus was for the purpose that men may be arrested and held in prison who cannot be proved guilty of any defined crime."

"A Marylander was seized by a party of soldiers and imprisoned in Fort McHenry. His friends asked Chief Justice Taney, of the Supreme Court, for a writ of habeas corpus which was granted, but the soldier said President Lincoln had authorized him to *suspend the writ*. Judge Taney said the President had no such power."

JUDGE BLACK, of Pennsylvania, in his *Essays*, says:

"A perfectly innocent and most respectable woman was lawlessly dragged from her family and brutally put to death, without judge or upon the mere order of certain military officers convoked for that purpose. It was, take it all in all, as foul a murder as ever blackened the face of God's sky. It was done in strict accordance with that 'Higher Law' and the Law Department of the United States approved it."

(See also Reverdy Johnson's testimony).

BARNES' *Popular History*, p. 597:

"Booth's accomplices were arrested, tried by a *military* court and convicted."

THE EXECUTION OF HENRY WIRZ.

"'He was tried out of his State by suborned witnesses— all witnesses in his defense were not permitted to be admitted to the stand—and judge and jury partial."

(See testimony of Louis Schade, his lawyer).

EXTRACTS taken from Page's *"True History of Andersonville"*:

"Major Wirz was the object of that popular injustice that personifies causes and demands victims for unpopular movements. All the accumulated passions of the war were concentrated upon this one man. He was the magnet that drew the Northern wrath to satiety."

"The South never believed that Wirz was guilty nor anybody else was guilty of the crimes alleged against him. The crimes could not have been committed without their knowledge. When, therefore, Captain Wirz, standing under the gallows and on the very brink of the grave, declared his innocence they believed he spoke the truth."

"The War Minister of the Government taking counsel of his passions, his prejudices and his hatreds, sought by the conviction and execution of Wirz to write a false chapter in the history of the war to infamize the South."

'One of the most truthful and reliable men of Georgia, an eminent surgeon, was summoned to Washington for the prosecution. Supposing that the Judge Advocate was desirous of getting *the truth,* went to him before the trial to tell him that the vaccine matter used upon the prisoners was the same that was used upon the women and children in the country, having been introduced into the South from abroad, and had the same effect upon the women and children as it had upon the prisoners.

"The Judge Advocate did not allude to this testimony when the witness was called to the stand, and when the counsel for defense recalled him to the stand to explain this matter, the Judge Advocate used all his legal ingenuity to prevent the truth being told."

"When one of the prisoners was called as a witness, he testified to a chapter of horrors, and on leaving the stand another prisoner accosted him and asked him why he had said those things, his reply was: 'I swore to a lie, and if I could return to the stand I would swear it all away."

"The military gentlemen who composed the commission with Mr. Stanton at their back have had their fleeting triumph. Wirz will have his in history. The day will yet come when they will deplore the parts they have played in this disreputable tragedy."

"He was doomed before he was heard, and even the permission to be heard according to law was denied him." (p. 236).

"On the evening before his execution some officers came to Wirz's Confessor, Father Boyle, and also to me—Louis Schade, his attorney, one of them informing me that a high Cabinet official wished to assure Wirz that if he would implicate Jefferson Davis with the atrocities committed at Andersonville, his sentence would be commuted. The messenger wished me to inform Wirz of this. In the presence of Father Boyle, I told Wirz this. His reply was, "Jefferson Davis had no connection with me as to what was done at Andersonville, and if I knew anything about him I would not become a traitor to save my life." (p. 237).

"All connected with Wirz have been released except Jefferson Davis. Now as Wirz could not conspire alone, nobody now, in view of this fact, considers him guilty."

History records that Henry Wirz could not be convicted on any charge brought against him.

> "I do not hesitate to assert that out of the 160 witnesses that testified, 145 declared that Captain Wirz never murdered or killed any Union prisoners with his own hands or otherwise." (p. 239).

No names of the alleged murdered men could ever be given, and when it was stated that a murder had been committed, no such prisoners could be found or identified. Those who were said to have died from wounds inflicted by Wirz in many cases lived five or six days, yet died nameless. This alone would testify to the falsity of the charges.

Louis Schade, Wirz's attorney:

> "Secretary Stanton denied Christian burial to Captain Wirz. He lies side by side with the remains of Mrs. Surratt, another and acknowledged victim of military commission in the yard of the former jail of this city."

Pa e's *History*, p. 247:

> "To my fellow prisoners that still insist that Captain Wirz was guilty and merited his tragic death: Do you know of your own personal knowledge that he ever maimed or killed a Union prisoner of war? Isn't it prejudice pure and simple, prejudice caused by your privations and sufferings at Andersonville? Could you have done better had you been in his place? I judge Henry Wirz from my personal knowledge of his character. Let us be fair about the matter."

M. L. Haley, No. 819 Fifth Avenue, Helena, Montana, says his friend, a prisoner at Andersonville, told him that the Henry Wirz that he knew at Andersonville, and the Henry Wirz tried at Washington were two different persons. He had charge of 100 men and he twice saw Wirz burst into tears when he saw the men suffering and he could not help them.

Some of the prisoners who were at Andersonville testify that Glazier's, Kellogg's, Spencer's, and Urban's histories of Andersonville are absolutely untruthful.

General O. H. LaGrange, of the Federal Army, said:

> "My personal observation of Wirz leaves no doubt in my mind that h e was sacrificed to meet the demands of a class of people who demanded his life to satisfy their revengeful spirit. I was summoned as a witness and saw the feeling underlying the fearful prosecution."

THE XIV. AND XV. AMENDMENTS.

HORTON says:

"The war changed the entire character and system of our government, overthrew the rights of States, and *forced amendments against the action of the people,* which made those amendments unconstitutional."

"Constitutional View of the War," Stephens, p. 15:

"The South claimed that the States under Reconstruction were *required* and literally compelled to form such constitutions as suited the dominant faction at Washington, and that while enfranchising the millions of blacks in our midst they denied the whites in those States the right to make Constitutions to secure safety and happiness."

Therefore, they regard both of those Amendments XIV. and XV. as unconstitutional.

THE CHICAGO CHRONICLE:

"The Fifteenth Amendment to the Constitution grew out of revenge, for the purpose of punishing the Southern people. It became a part of the Constitution by fraud and force to secure the results of war. The war was not fought to secure negro suffrage."

While Congress did not explicitly promise that it would admit the Representatives and Senators of the States which ratified the Fourteenth Amendment, it doubtless would have done so; but every one (except Sumner) was indignant at the disqualifying clause and overwhelmingly rejected the Amendment. It thus failed to secure the votes of three-fourths of the States of the Union for ratification.

Congress angered by this conduct on the part of the South, decided to take the reconstruction of the States entirely into is own hands. This was a violation of the Constitution.

"The United States shall guarantee to every State in the Union a Republican form of government, and shall protect each of them against invasion and domestic violence."

BLOCKADE.

The Federal government asserted that the seceding States were still in the Union—then how could they invade and destroy homes and property, and how blockade their ports?

"The blockade acknowledged the Confederacy a bellig-

erent power *outside of the Union;* since no nation can blockade its own ports. President Lincoln would never acknewl-
edge that the Southern States were out of.the Union, so
when he declared a blockade and England and France pro-
claimed neutrality between the belligerents he became
greatly stirred and truly, if the truth be known, this led to
his Emancipation Act.''   .

FREEDOM OF PRESS.

John Fremont:

"The administration has managed the war for personal
ends, and with incapacity and selfish disregard of Constitutional rights, with violation of personal liberty of the press."

DECISIONS OF THE SUPREME COURT.

Chas. Francis Adams, Jr.

"By the decision of the Supreme Court in the case of
Dred Scott, it would seem that the South has won every
point. It had demanded all for slavery, and had, at last,
received it from the supreme judicial tribunal of the land.
To interfere with slavery now would be to violate the supreme law. This decision puts the burden of good be-
havior on the North, for the South has always held that
decision was the supreme law of the land."

J. G. Holland's *"Life of Abraham Lincoln,"* p. 284:

"The South stood by the decisions of the Supreme Court
—the North did not and Lincoln did not. In 'his Inaugural
Address Lincoln said, 'If the decisions of the Supreme
Court are irrevocably fixed, then the people cease to be
their own masters, and practically resign their government
into the hands of that eminent tribunal."

Report From the Charleston Convention, 1860:

"The Southern representatives said that they would stand
by the Constitution and the decisions of the Supreme Court
whether for or against the South, and the Northern representatives refused to stand by the decisions of the Supreme
Court and the highest tribunal of the land."

Barnes' *"Popular History,"* p. 476, in the Dred Scott case:

"Judge Taney affirmed that negroes · were not citizens
and that Congress had no power under the Constitution to
forbid slavery in the Territories."

LINCOLN, in his Cooper Institute Speech, said:

· "In spite of Judge Taney's decision, Congress did have a right to prohibit slavery in the Territories."

SQUATTER SOVEREIGNTY.

VON HOLST, *"The Construction Construed"*:

"The Republican platform which elected Abraham Lincoln declared the Dred Scott decision a political heresy, the Missouri Compromise *unconstitutional* and Squatter Sovereignty *unconstitutional* because it allowed a territorial government to exclude slavery."

THE TRENT AFFAIR.

"On August 29, 1861, President Davis appointed James M. Mason, of Virginia, and John Sidell, of Louisiana, commissioners to England and France to place the Confederacy in the right light before these two great nations. They ran the blockade at Charleston, S. C., October 12, 1861, and proceeded to Havana, and sailed for Southampton, England, on the *Trent*, commanded by Captain Wilkes. The commissioners were taken from the ship with their secretaries and taken to Fort Warren to be imprisoned. The North highly approved of this act and the House of Representatives with the President's approval voted Captain Wilkes a gold medal. This was a direct violation of the International Law and England demanded their release and an apology. The United States government, through its representative, Mr. Seward, did both and did it quickly."

XIII.

Jefferson Davis Must Have His Rightful Place in History.

The United States government is indebted to Jefferson Davis for the following services:

Distinguished services in the Black Hawk War.

Served valiantly in the war with Mexico.

Hero at Monterey; wounded at Buena Vista; scaled the walls of the City of Mexico.

He introduced the wedge movement and saved the day at Buena Vista.

United States Senator from Mississippi.

Secretary of War in Pierce's Cabinet.

First to suggest trans-continental railroads connecting the Atlantic with the Pacific.

First to suggest camels as ships of the uninhabitable West to convey military stores.

First to suggest buying Panama Canal Zone.

First to suggest buying Cuba.

He planned American trade with China and Japan.

He suggested closer relations with South America.

He urged preparedness for war.

He enlarged the United States Army by four regiments.

He organized cavalry service adapted to our needs.

He introduced light infantry or rifle system of tactics.

He caused the manufacture of guns, rifles and pistols.

He rendered invaluable services to Colt's Armory.

He ordered the frontier surveyed.

He put young officers in training for surveying expeditions.

He sent George D. McClellan to Crimea to study the military tactics of the British and Russian armies.

He appointed Robert E. Lee as Superintendent of West Point.

He advanced Albert Sidney Johnston to important posts.

He had forts repaired and many of them rebuilt.

He strengthened forts on the Western frontier, frequently drawing on arsenals in the South to do it.

He had the Western part of the continent explored for scientific, geographical and railroad work.

He was responsible for the new Senate Hall, the new House of Representatives, and for the extension of many public buildings in Washington, especially the Treasury Building.

He was responsible for the construction of the aqueduct system in the Nation's capital.

He was responsible for "Armed Liberty" on the Capitol having a helmet of eagle feathers instead of the cap of a pagan goddess.

He had Cabin John Bridge built with its span of 220 feet.

He was United States Senator under President Buchanan.

He was nominated for President by Massachusetts men in 1860.

He refused to allow his name to be presented for President at the Charleston Convention.

He stood strongly for the Union, but stressed the constitutional right of a State to secede.

He did secede with Mississippi, as he had been taught at West Point.

He stood for what Lincoln preached but did not practice—"Not to overthrow the Constitution, but to overthrow the men who perverted the Constitution."

Nowhere did his genius display itself more signally than as Secretary of War under Franklin Pierce.

RECORDS OF WAR DEPARTMENT, Washington City:

"He revised the Army Regulations, showing a thorough knowledge of the subject and a matserful grasp of the needs of our army, as well as the armies of Europe.

"That he believed in preparedness is shown by the fact that he insisted upon the addition of four regiments to the army and organized a cavalry service peculiarly adapted to the wants of the country; introduced light infantry, or the rifle system of tactics, and caused the manufacture of rifles, muskets and pistols. He gave such valuable suggestions to workmen at Colt's Armory that they made him a pistol on the silver breech of which they engraved the words: 'To a brother inventor.'

"Through his influence numberless forts were repaired and rehabilitated, the frontier defences strengthened, and the Wetsern part of the continent explored for scientific, geographical and railroad purposes. It is with pride we look back upon his work in the Coast Survey question, for he was recognized as the ablest and best posted defender in this work. Under the supervision of the War Department, during the first year of Mr. Davis' service, the extension of the new Capitol was energetically prosecuted. He stood by General Meigs in all his efforts to construct the waterworks, finish the Capitol building on the grandest scale, and to push forward the extension of the Treasury Department. A splendid stone aqueduct, which spans 220 feet, a few miles from Washington, built during Mr. Davis' term as Secretary of War, still remains a monument to his earnest labor for the benefit of the capitol. It is known as 'Cabin John Bridge.' "

IN EWING'S book, "Northern Rebellion Against the Constitution Producing Southern Secession," he shows up Kansas in her true light:

"The fight against the South crystallized in Kansas. The rebellion was open against the government, and Jefferson Davis, when Secretary of War, had to put down that rebellion and restore peace and order. John Brown reopened the fight in Kansas, later taking it to Harper's Ferry.''

A tribute from one of the North who served with Davis in the War with Mexico is:

"Fellow citizens: I was at Buena Vista. I saw the battle lost and victory in the grasp of the brutal and accursed foe. I saw the favorite son of 'Harry of the West,' my colonel, weltering in his blood as he died on the field. I saw death or captivity worse than death in store for every Kentuckian on that gory day. Everything seemed lost and was hopeless when a Mississippi regiment with Jefferson Davis at its head appeared on the scene. I see him now as he was then—the incarnation of battle, the avatar of rescue. He turned the tide; he snatched victory from defeat: he saved the army; his heroic hand wrote 'Buena Vista' in letters of everlasting glory on our proud escutcheon, a hero, my countryman, my brother, my rescuer. He is no less so this day, and I would strike the shackles from his aged limbs and make his as free as the vital air of heaven, and clothe him with every right I enjoy, had I the power.''

CONGRESSIONAL RECORDS: On May 24, 1850, Jefferson Davis, of Mississippi, in the Senate of the United States passed a set of resolutions containing this extract:

"Any intermeddling of any one or more States by a combination of citizens with the domestic institutions of other States, on any pretext, whatever, political, moral, or religious, with a view of disturbance in violation of the Constitution, is insulting to the States so interfered with and tends to weaken the Union.''

The Resolutions passed 36 to 19. Eight States refused to vote and these eight States were the ones that had nullified the Fugitive Slave law and later elected Abraham Lincoln President. The South knew this and resented Lincoln's election.

His speech as Fanueil Hall, Boston, 1853, was a masterly effort in defence of the South and the Constitutional right of slavery. When it was known that he was to make his *Farewell Address* to the Senate in 1861, the House of Representatives came in a body to hear him.

It was at West Point he studied Rawle's "*View of the Constitution,*" which taught him that if a State seceded—showing that it was an acknowledged fact by the Constitution that a State had the right to secede—the duty of a soldier reverted to his State—hence Davis, Robert E. Lee, Thomas J. Jackson, the

Johnstons and others, acting upon this instruction, cast their lot with their States in 1861. Thus it happened that when in 1865 the question of a trial of Jefferson Davis was agitated, Chief Justice Chase said that a trial would condemn the North, and so no trial was ever held. He was released on bail but his political disabilities were never removed.

JEROME E. TITLOW, the one sent to manacle him, said:

"Upon him criticism expended all its arrows and yet no blemish was found."

Men who did not love him or admire him as a politician were forced to acknowledge. his fine traits of character.

NEW YORK WORLD:

"Jefferson Davis was a man of commanding ability, spotless integrity, controlling conscience, and a temper so resolute that at times it approached obstinacy. He was proud, sensitive and honorable in all his dealings and in every relation of life."

THE EDITOR of the *New York Sun* said:

"Amid irreparable disaster, Jefferson Davis was sustained by a serene consciousness that he had done a man's work according to his lights, and that, while unable to command success, he had striven to deserve it. Even among those who looked upon him with least sympathy it was felt that he bore defeat and humiliation in the highest Roman fashion."

CHARLES FRANCIS ADAMS, JR.:

"No fatal mistakes either of administration or strategy were made which can be fairly laid to his account. He did the *best possible* with the means that he had at his command. Merely the opposing forces were too many and too strong for him. Of his austerity, earnestness and fidelity there can be no more question that can be entertained of his capacity."

DR. CRAVEN, his prison physician, gave this testimony:

"The more I saw of him the more I was convinced of his sincere religious convictions. He impressed me more with the divine origin of God's Word than any professor. of Christianity I ever met."

Did his Christianity extend to forgiveness of his enemies. A Northern man, Ridpath, the historian, a guest at Beauvoir, testified that during his visit he never heard one word of bitterness toward any man. A quotation from a speech made to the Mississippi Legislature March 10, 1884, will in itself suffice to answer this question:

> "Our people have accepted that decree; it therefore behooves them, as they may, to promote the general welfare of the Union, to show to the world that hereafter as heretofore, the patriotism of our people is not measured by lines of latitude and longitude, but is as broad as the obligations they have assumed and embraces the whole of our ocean-bound domain. Let them leave to their children's children the good example of never swerving from the path of duty, and *prefering* to *return good for evil rather than to cherish the unmanly feeling of revenge.*"

When the news came that Lee must fall back from Petersburg, which meant the evacuation of Richmond, and a possible surrender, he was found on his knees in prayer in St. Paul's Church, Richmond, Va.

Did Jefferson Davis ever regret the step that was taken in regard to secession?

> "It has been said that I should apply to the United States for a pardon; but repentance must precede the right of pardon, and I have not repented. Remembering, as I must, all which has been suffered, all which has been lost, disappointed hopes, and crushed aspirations, yet I deliberately say, if it were to do over again, I would do just as I did in 1861.
>
> "Never teach your children to admit that their fathers were wrong in their effort to maintain the sovereignty, freedom and independence which was their inalienable birthright. I cannot believe that the causes for which our sacrifices were made can ever be lost, but rather hope that those who now deny the justice of our asserted claims will learn from experience that the fathers builded wisely and the Constitution should be construed according to the commentaries of those men who made it."

CHIEF JUSTICE CHASE:

> "If Jefferson Davis be brought to trial it will convict the North and exonerate the South."

II.

CHARLES O'CONNOR:

"Rawle's *'View of the Constitution'* and Bledsoe's *'Is Davis a Traitor?'*, would have won the case without further testimony had it come to trial." (The Trial of Jefferson Davis).

On page 44 of *"The Republic of Republics,"* is found this statement:

"A solemn consultation of a small number of the ablest lawyers of the North was held in Washington to discuss the question whether the Federal Government should commence a criminal prosecution against Jefferson Davis for his participation and leadership in the War of Secession. The council was conducted with the utmost secrecy. Among those present were Attorney-General Speed, Judge Clifford Wm. Evarts, and perhaps a dozen others who had been selected from the whole Northern profession for their legal ability and acumen, and the result of their deliberation was the sudden abandonment of the idea of prosecution in view of the insurmountable difficulties of securing conviction."

Charles O'Connor, one of Mr. Davis' counsel and one of the most distinguished lawyers in the United States, after reading the lines of argument by Dr. Bledsoe in *"Is Davis a Traitor?"* wrote to him that with so admirably prepared, and overwhelmingly conclusive brief as was contained in his book, his task of defending Mr. Davis would be easy indeed.

REV. DR. BACON, of Assonet, Massachusetts, said:

"While the trial of Mr. Davis was pending, Mr. Wm. B. Reed, one of the counsel for defence, was a member of my brother's congregation at Orange, N. J. He told my brother that if the case had come to trial, Rawle's *'View of the Constitution,'* the textbook from which Davis had been instructed at West Point, would have been used in his defense, and when this was learned, it was decided the trial was not to take place." (See *North American Review,* September, 1904).

Charles Francis Adams testified that before Story's *Commentaries* were published in 1833, Rawle's *'View of the Constitution,'* (published in 1825) was the textbook at West Point, and continued in use up to 1840.

R. G. Horton, in his *"Youth's History of the Civil War,"* published in 1868, on page 384, says:

> "It is extremely doubtful whether the abolitionists will ever dare to bring Mr. Davis before a fair tribunal; for in that case they would themselves be proved the traitors and rebels which they accuse him of being. Probably under some pretext he will be allowed liberty and thus end the last act in the four years tragedy of sorrow.
>
> "His counsel demanded a speedy trial knowing he would be vindicated. The Federal Government postponed the trial three years. When, at last, the case was called Chief Justice Chase blocked the prosecution by some technical point and referred the decision to the Supreme Court; and that case, today, rests on the Supreme Court docket never to be brought to trial—what does this prove? It completely vindicates the *man* and the *cause.*"

In 1876, eleven years after the South surrendered, Mr. James G. Blaine of Maine, stood up in Congress and poured out "a lot of hate-born lies as malignant as human tongue ever uttered or human brain ever concocted:"

> "Mr. Davis," cried Mr. Blaine, "was the author, knowingly, deliberately, guiltily, and willfully, of the gigantic murders and crimes at Andersonville. And I here before God, measuring my words, knowing their full intent, and import, declare that neither the deeds of the Duke of Alva in the Low Country, nor the massacre of St. Bartholomew, nor the thumb screws, and other engine of torture of the Inquisition, begin to compare in atrocity with the hideous crimes of Andersonville."

Mr. Hill's reply:

> "If nine per cent. of the men in Southern prisons were starved and tortured to death by Mr. Jefferson Davis, who tortured to death the twelve per cent. of the Southern men who died in Northern prisons?" (See "Secretary Stanton's Statistics."

Judge Shea was sent in 1866 to Canada to examine the secret sessions' records of the Confederate Government. Through the courtesy of General John C. Breckenridge, Judge Shea was allowed to examine these records, especially those in regard to the care of and exchange of prisoners. This was taken from Judge Shea's report:

> "It was decisively manifest that Mr. Davis steadily and unflinchingly set himself in opposition to the demands for

retaliation, and this impaired his personal influence and brought censure upon him from Southern people. These secret sessions show that Mr. Davis strongly desired to do something which would secure better treatment of his men in Northern prisons; and would place the war on the footing of wars waged by people in modern times, and divest it of a savage character. Mr. Davis never did yield to the continual demand for retaliation.''

RUSSELL's *Diary*, p. 163; Correspondence to *London Times:*

"The stories which have been so sedulously spread of the barbarity and cruelty of the Confederates to all the wounded Union men ought to be set at rest by the printed statements of the eleven Union surgeons, just released, who have come back from Richmond, where they were sent after their capture on the field of Bull Run, with the most distinct testimony that the Confederates treated their prisoners with humanity. Who are the miscreants who assert that the rebels burned the wounded in hospitals and bayoneted them as they lay helpless on the battlefield?''

EDITOR of the New Haven (Conn.) *Register* says:

"There is something to say about Jefferson Davis and his admission to the Hall of Fame. It is high time it was said. It is high time that the mist which for half a century has distorted the North's view of this son of the South was cleared away. It is in justice time that the man, who in his day suffered more than any other Southerner for the cause in which he believed, should cease to be reckoned a traitor and a coward and be esteemed for what he was, a brave, true Southern gentleman. . . . . . The South will never cease to admire the man of iron nerve, of dauntless courage. of ceaseless loyalty, of unsullied honor, of tireless energy, of peerless chivalry, who suffered and dared and all but died for the cause he loved and lost. Of that host of true men who gave their best and their all for the Confederacy because in their deepest hearts they believed they were doing right, none was more sincere than he. Of that multitude who lined up for the struggle against their brothers of the North, none was braver, none was nobler. His sacrifice was as extreme as it was sincere, and his treatment by the victors after the crash came was sore medicine for a heart that was breaking. . . . . .

"What better time could there be to signify. by the placing of his statue in the nation's capital, that the wounds of that war are healed, that in the blood of brothers shed the Union is forever cemented on a foundation that standeth sure? Then let his presentment stand erect, noble, commanding, impressive as he stood in the days when he was master of the destinies of half a nation. . . . . . Let it picture a martyr to a cause that, though lost, was not wholly vain, since it taught brothers to appreciate a relationship they were in danger of forgetting. And not inappropriately might there be carved on it the inscription which an unknown poet of the South once suggested for his statue:

> " 'Write on its base, 'We loved him.' All these years
> Since that torn flag was folded we've been true,
> The love that bound us now revealed in tears
> Like webs unseen till heavy with the dew.' "

The writer of this article knew Mr. Davis personally, and in his home at Beauvoir was his guest. In addition, he had also been one of his escort from Charlotte, N. C., to Washington, Ga. In the home of Mr. Davis no word of bitterness toward even those who had despitefully used him was heard. He declined to discuss the politics of the day, evidently feeling the indignity that was daily heaped upon him by those who, forgetting nothing, also learned nothing. Of Mr. Lincoln he spoke several times in kindly terms, instancing his fine capacity for illustrating his meaning with apt anecdotes, an accomplishment in which he thought few public men had excelled him. Though in Congress at the same time as Mr. Lincoln, he stated that he had no recollection of his personality. In an article which was written by the writer of this after his visit to Mr. Davis the following is found:

> "Not by word or tone did this chief of the greatest of civil wars express other than respect for the memory of that other great Kentuckian who, like himself, sat in a Presidential chair and held in his hands the destinies of a great people during that struggle between the two finest armies of volunteers the world has ever known."

POLK JOHNSON, "*Confederate Veteran*," Louisville, Ky., January, 1920:

> "The most remarkable man of his day in many respects, the chief of the greatest civil war the world has known, the head of a government and army which, considering their resources, or the lack of them, put on record the greatest military achievements of the age; the unfaltering advocate of an idea which he refuses to abandon in the face of defeat, which idea represents the opinions of the found-

ers of the government and the spirit of the Constitution, he sits by the side of the sea, a citizen of no land under the sun; proscribed, misrepresented, and·derided, yet accepting it all without a murmur and calmly resting his case for those who will come after all of us to decide, conscious of the uprightness of his public and private career, his faithful devotion to his State and section, and the honesty of his purposes. Surrounded by his family, he as calmly and bravely awaits the end, which cannot be far away now, as he faced the storm of Santa Anna's bullets in Mexico and bore the indignity of chains and the horrors of a dungeon in later years. Kindly, gentle old man! When that good gray head is pillowed upon the bosom of your beloved Mississippi, may there come one who will write upon the pages of history the fair record of your brave, upright, and honored life, for it has been and is all of these, deny it as your bitterest adversary may!''

''In vain Mr. Davis requested to be taken into open court. They would not for they knew they had no particle of evidence on which to convict him. Were he tried for Lincoln's murder, Judge Shea and Horace Greeley would testify that *they* would be proved guilty of lying not Mr. Davis of murder. If tried for treason not Mr. Davis but the whole of the Republican party would be tried for treason. and Chief Justice Chase would testify to this. If tried for cruelty at Andersonville, Chas. Dana would testify to the falsity of this charge—yet the Federal government kept Mr. Davis in prison two years, and every day after for a dozen or more years the Republican party continued to pour on Mr. Davis' name streams of sulphuric hate.''

His servants were greatly attached to him. He was always just to them. When he died they wrote to Mrs. Davis:

''We, the old servants of our beloved master, have cause to mingle our tears over his death. He was always so kind and thoughtful of our peace and happiness. We extend our humble sympathy.''

JOHN P. SJOLANDER:

''*And when the mists are blown from 'round the height*
On which he lived. perchance some noble mind,
Born in that newer day and clearer light.
Up to its peak shall point out to mankind
The long white road he trod alone at night.''

XIV.

Abraham Lincoln Must Have His Rightful Place in History.

AUTHORITY:

Summed up, the services of Lincoln to the United States government were:

Captain in the Black Hawk War.

One term in the House of Representatives, 1846.

Elected President of the United States by the Republican party on a minority vote.

Re-elected President in 1865, over McClellan, by using his power as commander-in-chief of the army.

He involved the United States in war by re-enforcing Fort Sumter.

In the ''Trent'' affair he came very near involving the United States in war with England.

He refused to aid Mexico against Maxmilian in 1863, and thus kept the United States out of war.

He freed the slaves of the Southern States by a proclamation that was unconstitutional.

He preserved the Union, not by a constitutional right, but by armed might.   (George Lunt, Herndon, Lamon, McClellan).

"Lincoln signed the liquor revenue bill and turned the saloons loose on the country, thus undoing the previous temperance work of the churches."

"He studied men more than he studied books. He knew their strong points, and their weak points; he knew their faults, their foibles, their whims and their caprices.

"He had few friends and fewer intimates. He unbosomed himself to none. He responded quickly to distress. He was physically and morally brave. His will was immovable yet he was the child of policy and expediency. He was ambitious and aspiring. He was self-confident and never hesitated to cross mental swords with the most brilliant.

"His real strength lay in knowing plain people for he was one of them, and there are more plain people in the world than any other kind. He saw their struggle and toil, their griefs and tears. He knew how they thought and felt and acted. He was their friend and they knew it. He knew how to communicate with them in their speech and amuse them by his jokes. He was an American, but an American of a new national type."

GEORGE LUNT says:

"Lincoln was incapable of wide range of thought. He was infirm of purpose led by sharper minds. He frequently insisted upon minor points of consideration whether right or wrong. A large majority of the people had never heard of him before his nomination."

"He has been compared to Washington, but his loosely constituted and indecisive character cannot be compared to the high-toned and sagacious Washington." (*"Origin of Late War,"* p. 435.

"Mr. Lincoln was elected by the States not the people. He received the majority of electoral votes but was nearly one and a half million of votes in minority counting the votes of the people. Although Mr. Lincoln was elected by State rights yet he went to work at once to destroy State rights.

"He had a way of illustrating by anecdote what his wishes were thus not openly committing himself to anything that could politically be brought against him.

"By an anecdote he let Grant know that his terms of surrender for Lee must be magnanimous. By an anecdote he showed very plainly he desired President Davis to escape and not fall into the hands of the North. He knew Davis could never be tried for treason, therefore, he did not wish the test made. Had he lived, Sherman's terms of surrender to Johnston would not have been so severely dealt with by the Cabinet, for those were the very terms Lincoln would have wished, because of his injustice to the South.

"His death was the greatest blow that could have befallen the South. Jefferson Davis said this, Howell Cobb and other Southern statesmen said this. No statesmen, North or South, rejoiced over the news of his death except Thad Stevens who desired to carry out his own Reconstruction policy instead of Lincoln's.

"He realized that he would be obliged to free all slaves by war, so he planned a bill to introduce into Congress to pay $400,000,000 for slaves belonging to the slaveholders of the North. He realized how this act of coercion which brought on the war and his freeing of the slaves, and destruction and confiscation of the life and property of the Southern States had been caused by the acts of war, so his policy for Reconstruction was made as magnanimous as he dared or could be expected."

GODWIN, of *"The Nation,"* says:

"The first real breach in the Constitution was President Lincoln's using his war power to abolish slavery."

THAD STEVENS:

"I will not stultify myself by supposing that Mr. Lincoln has any warrant in the Constitution for dismembering Virginia."

McCLURE, his friend, said:

"Mr. Lincoln swore to obey the Constitution, but in eighteen months violated it by his Emancipation Proclamation."

MR. RHODES (Vol. IV., p. 213), says:

"There was no authority for the Proclamation by the Constitution and laws—nor was there any statute that warranted it."

Mr. Lincoln in all fairness must be judged by the truth of history alone as recorded by the men of the North—those who placed him in power. The evidence is very strong against him as *a violator of the Constitution.*

WENDELL PHILLIPS, at the Cooper Institute, 1864, said:

"I judge Mr. Lincoln by his acts, his violations of the law, his overthrow of liberty in the Northern States.

"I judge Mr. Lincoln by his words, his deeds, and so judging him, I am unwilling to trust Abraham Lincoln with the future of this country."

PERCY GREGG said:

"Lincoln's order that Confederate commissions or letters of marque granted to private or public ships should be disregarded and their crews treated as pirates, and all medicines declared contraband of war, violated every rule of civilized war and outraged the conscience of Christendom."

"Lincoln never hesitated to violate the Constitution when he so desired. The Chief Justice testified to this. Lincoln suspended the Writ of Habeas Corpus in 1861; he allowed West Virginia to be formed from Virginia contrary to the Constitution; he issued his Emancipation Proclamation without consulting his Cabinet and in violation of the Constitution."

"He consented to a cartel for exchange of prisoners February, 14. 1862. When it was to the advantage of the North, faith was kept; when it was to the advantage of the

South, it was violated." (See Cor. Lieut. Col. Ludlow and Col. Ould, July 26, 1863).

"Had he been humane, he would not have allowed 38,000 men and women—editors, politicians, clergymen of good character and honor—imprisoned in gloomy, damp casements, for no overt act, but simply because they were 'Democrat suspects.'" (*"Life and Times of Hannibal Hamlin,"* p. 393). (Bancroft's *"Life of Seward,"* Vol. 2, p. 254).

BOUTWELL, Congressman from Massachusetts, said:

"With varying degrees of intensity the whole Democratic party sympathized with the South and arraigned Lincoln and the Repulican party for all the country endured."

"On Circuit With Lincoln," p. 364:

"Lincoln was not in any sense of the word an *Abolitionist.* He had no intention to make voters of negroes—in fact their welfare did not enter into his policy at all."

TARBELL:

"Mr. Chase was never able to see Mr. Lincoln's greatness."

McCLURE:

"Chase was the most irritating fly in the Lincoln ointment."

RHODES, Vol. IV., p. 320:

"Lincoln's contemporaries failed to perceive his greatness."

"Ben Wade and Henry W. Davis issued a manifesto against him. Sumner, Wade, Davis, and Chase were his 'malicious foes.' Lincoln was forced to appoint Chase to the office of Chief Justice in order to remove him from the Cabinet, for he was said to be 'the irritating fly in the Lincoln ointment.' Stanton called Lincoln 'a coward and a fool.' Seward said he had 'a cunning that amounted to genius.' Richard Dana said, 'The lack of respect for the President by his Cabinet cannot be concealed.' He was called 'the baboon at the other end of the avenue,' and 'the idiot of the White House.' Had not Grant succeeded in gaining a victory at Vicksburg, a movement to appoint a Dictator in Lincoln's place would have gone into effect. His Cabinet had lost confidence in his policy."

BENJAMIN R. CURTIS, of the Supreme Court ("Executive Power") says:

"The President has made himself a legislator. He has

enacted penal laws governing citizens of the United States. He has super-added to his rights as commander the power of usurper. He has established a military despotism. He can now use the authority he has assumed to make himself master of our lives, our liberties, our properties, with power to delegate his mastership to such satraps as he may select."

IDA TARBELL'S *"Life of Lincoln":*

"In the winter of 1862-'63 many and many a man deserted the army. They refusel to fight. Mr. Lincoln knew that hundreds of soldiers were being urged by parents and friends to desert. New York, Pennsylvania, Ohio, Indiana and Illinois reserved their vote. The people were weary of war, weary of so much waste of life and money. Open dissatisfaction was shown in Pennsylvania and Wisconsin which broke out in violence over the draft for more men."

JOHN A. LOGAN, *"Great Conspiracy,"* p. 551, Springfield, Ill., June, 1863:

"There was open and avowed hosttility to Lincoln in Philadelphia, New York, Boston and strong opposition in New Jersey. So violent was the hostility to war in Massachusetts and New York, the call of volunteers was unheeded, and when the government demanded a draft, the people gathered in crowds and fearful riots ensued. In New York City the opposition was so violent, the rioters so numerous, the city was terrified for days and nights. The houses in which the draft machines were at work were wrecked and then burned -to ashes. The order for draft was rescinded by the government at Washington and the people urged to disperse and to retire to their homes on the promise that there would be no more drafting."

IDA TARBLL, p. 165, *McClure's Magazine,* January, 1893:

"Many and many a man deserted in the winter of 1862-'63, because of Lincoln's Emancipation Proclamation. The soldiers did not believe that Lincoln had the right to issue it, and they refused to fight. Lincoln knew that hundreds were deserting."

B. T. BUTLER says:

"During the whole war the Lincoln government was rarely aided, but was unanimously impeded by the decisions of the Supreme Court, so that President Lincoln was obliged to suspend the Writ of Habeas Corpus in order to relieve himself from the rulings of the Court."

TARBELL'S *"Life of Lincoln":*

"It was declared that Lincoln had violated Constitutional rights, declared that he had violated personal liberty, and the liberty of the press. It was said that Lincoln had been guilty of all the abuses of a military dictatorship. Much bitter criticism was made of his treatment of the South's peace commissioners. The despair, the indignation of the country centered on Mr. Lincoln."

MORSE, *"American Statesmen":*

"Many distinguished men of his own party distrusted him."

RICHARD A. DANA, (Letters to Thomas Lathrop), February 23, 1863:

"I see no hope but in the army; the lack of respect for the President in all parties is unconcealed. He has no admirers. If a convention were held tomorrow he would not get the vote of a single state."

WENDELL PHILLIPS:

"As long as you keep the present turtle (Mr. Lincoln) at the head of affairs you make a pit with one hand, and fill it with the other."

WENDELL PHILLINS:

"The re-election of Abraham Lincoln will be National destruction."

MCCLURE:

"It is an open secret that Stanton advised the overthrow of the Lincoln government to be replaced by McClellan as military dictator."

HAPGOOD'S *"Life of Lincoln":*

"Charles A. Dana testifies that the whole power of the War Department was used to secure Lincoln's re-election in 1864. There is no doubt that this is true. Purists may turn pale at such things, but the world wants no prettified portrait of Mr. Lincoln's Jesuitical ability to use the fox's skin when the lion's proves too short and that was one part of his enormous value."

RICHARD H. DANA, March, 1863, in a letter to Charles Francis Adams, Sr., Minister to England, said:

"If a Republican Convention was to be held tomorrow he would not get the vote of a single state. He is an unspeakable calamity to us where he is."

LAMON'S *"Life of Lincoln":*

"No phase of Mr. Lincoln's character has been so persistently misrepresented as this of his religious belief."

HERNDON'S *"Life of Lincoln":*

"Abraham Lincoln became more discreet in later life and used words and phrases to make it appear that he was a Christian. He never changed on this subject. He lived and died a deep-grounded infidel."

LAMON'S *"Life of Lincoln":*

"Mr. Lincoln went to church, but he went to mock and came away to mimic."

HAPGOOD'S *"Life of Lincoln,"* p. 183:

"All the clergy in Springfield voted against Lincoln."

LAMON:

"The people all drank, and Abe was for doing what the people did, right or wrong."

E. C. INGERSOLL:

"President Lincoln is now clothed with power as full as that of the Czar of Russia."

HENRY WARD BEECHER:

"I know it is said that President Lincoln is not the government; that the Constitution is the government. What! A sheep-skin parchment a government. President Lincoln and his Cabinet is now the government."

VIEWS ON SLAVERY.

LINCOLN said, (Hapgood's *"Abraham Lincoln, The Man of The People,"* p. 273):

"If I could save the Union without freeing any slaves I would do it."

ALLEN THORNDIKE RICE says, (*"Reminiscences of Lincoln,"* p. 14):

"Lincoln did not free the negro for the sake of the slave, but for the sake of the Union. It is an error to class him with the noble band of Abolitionists to whom neither church nor state were sacred when it sheltered slavery."

HERNDON, Lincoln's law partner:

"When Lovejoy the zealous Abolitionist came to Springfield to speak against slavery, Lincoln left town to avoid taking sides either for or against Abolition.''

LINCOLN said:

"Slaves are property, and if freed should be paid for.''

We cannot hold him up as a *hater of slavery*. Abraham Lincoln did not free the slaves because he hated slavery, nor for any love for the African race, nor for any desire to give them suffrage or social equality. In his campaign speeches, he said he had no thought of freeing the slaves. In his Inaugural Address he said the same. He made Hunter and Fremont in Missouri countermand their acts freeing the slaves in conquered territory in the early years of the war, saying, "they could not by the Constitution do it,'' and "the war was not being fought with any view of freeing the slaves.''

Congress had declared to Benjamin Franklin and to the Quakers that it had no right to free the slaves. The Constitution had not been amended, but Lincoln approved an act in 1861 which said "Congress had the right to abolish slavery in the States'' and this allowed the Constitution to be violated again.

Mr. Lincoln was an adroit politician. When dealing with the South, he said:

"I have no Constitutional right to free your slaves, and no desire to do so.''

When dealing with the Border States, he said:

"Slavery is not to be interfered with.''

When dealing with the Republican party, he said:

"This country cannot remain half slave and half free.''

When dealing with the Abolitionists, he said:

"This war is against slavery.''

When dealing with Foreign Nations, he said:

"The slaves must be emancipated.''—Lunt.

He said he had no desire to free the slaves.—(Inaugural Address).

He said he had no Constitutional right to free them.—(Inaugural Address).

He said if freed they should be segregated.—(Butler's Works).

He said he never desired nor intended to give them political nor social equality.—(Butler's Works).

LINCOLN'S PROMISES.

INAUGURAL ADDRESS:

"Apprehension seems to exist among the people of the Southern States that by the accession of a Republican administration their property and their peace and personal security are to be endangered. There has never been any reasonable cause for such apprehension.

"I have no purpose directly or indirectly to interfere with the institution of slavery in the States where it exists. I believe I have no lawful right to do so, and I have no inclination to do so."

In his letter to Alexander Stephens, who wrote expressing his sympathy for him in the great responsibility resting upon him as President in those perilous days, he said:

("For your eye only.")

"Do the people of the South really entertain fear that a Republican administration would *directly* or *indirectly* interfere with their slaves, or with them about their slaves? If they do, I wish to assure you as once a friend, and still, I hope, not an enemy, that there is no cause for such fears. The South would be in no more danger in this respect than it was in the days of Washington." (*"Public and Private Letters of Alexander Stephens,"* p. 150).

VIEWS ON COLONIZATION OF THE NEGRO.

President Lincoln in his Emancipation Proclamation evidently had in mind to colonize or segregate the slaves if freed.

"It is my purpose to colonize persons of African descent, with their consent, upon this continent or elsewhere, with the previously obtained consent of the government existing there."

"From the time of his election as President he was striving to find some means of colonizing the negroes. An experiment had been made of sending them to Liberia, but it was a failure, and he wished to try another colony, hoping that would be successful. He sent one colony to Cow Island under Koch as overseer, but he proved very cruel to the negroes and they begged to return. He then asked for an appropriation of money from Congress to purchase land in Central America, but Central America refused to sell and said, 'Do not send the negroes here.' The North said, 'Do not send the negroes here.'

"It was agreed then that a Black Territory should be set apart for the segregation of the negroes in Texas, Mississippi and South Carolina—but Lincoln was unhappy, and in despair—he asked Ben Butler's advice, saying:

" 'If we turn 200,000 armed negroes in the South, among their former owners, from whom we have taken their arms, it will inevitably lead to a race war. It cannot be done. The negroes must be gotten rid of. Ben Butler said: 'Why not send them to Panama to dig the canal?' (See Butler's Book).

Lincoln was delighted at the suggestion, and asked Butler to consult Seward at once. Only a few days later John Wilkes Booth assassinated Lincoln and one of his conspirators wounded Seward. What would have been the result had Lincoln lived cannot be estimated. The poor negroes would possibly have been sent to that place of yellow fever and malarial dangers to perish from the face of the earth,.for we had no Gorgas of Alabama to study our sanitary laws for them at that time.

VIEWS ON SOCIAL EQUALITY OF THE NEGRO.

In his speech at Charleston, Ill., 1858, Lincoln said:

"I am not now, nor ever have been in favor of bringing about in any way the social or political equality of the white and black races. I am not now nor ever have been in favor of making voters or jurors of negroes, nor of qualifying them to hold office, nor of intermarriages with white people. There is a physical difference between the white and the black races which will forever forbid the two races living together on social or political equality. There must be a position of superior and inferior, and *I am in favor of assigning the superior position to the white man.*"

MUZZEY'S *"American History,"* p. 486. (Dr. Muzzey is the teacher of history at Columbia College, New York):

"Lincoln had no idea of forcing the South to give a single slave political rights."

In his speech at Peoria, Ill., he said:

"We know that some Southern men do free their slaves, go North and become tip-top abolitionists, while some Northern men go South and become most cruel masters.

"When Southern people tell us that they are no more responsible for the origin of slavery than we are, I acknowledge the fact. When it is said the institution exists, and it is very difficult to get rid of in any satisfactory way, I can understand and appreciate the saying. I surely will not

blame them for not doing what I should not know how to
do myself. If all earthly power were given me, I should
not know what to do as to the existing institution. My
first impulse would possibly be to free all the slaves and
send them to Liberia to their own native land. But a moment's reflection would convince me that this would not
be best for them. If they were all landed there in a day
they would all perish in the next ten days, and there is not
surplus money enough to carry them there in many times
ten days. What then? Free them all and keep them among
us as underlings. Is it quite certain that this would alter
their condition? Free them and make them politically
and socially our equals? My own feelings will not admit
of this, and if mine would, we well know that those of the
great mass of whites will not. We cannot make them our
equals. A system of gradual emancipation might be adopted, and I will not undertake to judge our Southern friends
for tardiness in this matter.''

"At Peoria ,Ill., in 1854, he said: 'I acknowledge the
constitutional rights of the States—not grudgingly, but
fairly and fully, and I will give them any legislation for
reclaiming their fugitive slaves.'

"The point the Republican party wanted to stress was
to oppose making slave States out of the newly acquired
territory, not abolishing slavery as it then existed. Lincoln
spoke of anti-slavery men in 1862 as 'Radicals and Abo
litionists.' Rhodes said that the abolitionists said, 'The
President is not with us; he has no anti-slavery instincts.' ''
(Rhodes' "History of United States," Vol. IV., p. 64).

EMANCIPATION.

GEORGE LUNT says:

"Emancipation is not within the scope of the Constitu-
tution, or in any degree at the disposition of the United
States government, and can mean nothing else than revolution for which the abolitionists are striving. Revolution
can only be justified by oppression and the power of oppression is not with the South."

MORSE'S "Abraham Lincoln," Vol. II., p. 102:

"I felt that measures otherwise unconstitutional might
become lawful by becoming indispensable. Right or wrong,
I assume this ground and now avow it."

CARPENTER repeats the President's words:

"I put the draft of the Proclamation aside, waiting for
a victory. Finally came the week of Antietam. I determined to wait no longer. I was then staying at the Sol-

diers' Home. Here I finished writing the second draft of the proclamation; called the Cabinet together to hear it, and it was published the following Monday. I made a solemn vow before God that if General Lee was driven back from Maryland I would crown the result by the declaration of freedom to the slaves." (Barnes' "*Popular History,*" Chap. XV.)

RHODES' "*History of the United States,*" Vol. IV., p. 344:

"His Emancipation Proclamation was not issued from a humane standpoint. He hoped it would incite the negroes to rise against the women and children."

"His Emancipation Proclamation was intended only as a punishment for the seceding States. It was with no thought of freeing the slaves of more than 300,000 *slaveholders then in the Northern army.*

"His Emancipation Proclamation was issued for a fourfold purpose and it was issued with fear and trepidation lest he should offend his Northern constituents. He did it:

FIRST:

"Because of an oath—that if Lee should be driven from Maryland he would free the slaves. (Barnes and Guerber).

SECOND:

"The time of enlistment had expired for many men in the army and he hoped this would encourage re-enlistment.

THIRD:

"Trusting that Southern men would be forced to return home to protect their wives and children from negro insurrection.

FOURTH:

"Above all he issued it to prevent foreign nations from recognizing the Confederacy."

RHODES, Vol. IV.:

"The House of Lords was almost unanimously for the South, as was the majority of the House of Commons, elected in that day by about a million voters."

WENDELL PHILLIPS:

"Lincoln was badgered into emancipation. After he issued it, he said it was the greatest folly of his life. It was like the Pope's bull against the comet."

Was he satisfied with its effect? Let us see what happened.

"*McClure's Magazine,*" January, 1893, p. 165; also Tarbell:

"Many and many a man deserted in the winter of 1862-'63 because of Lincoln's Emancipation Proclamation. The soldiers did not believe that Lincoln had the right to issue it. They refused to fight.''

WENDELL PHILLIPS said:

"Lincoln acknowledged that the Emancipation Proclamation was the greatest folly of his life.''

NICOLAY & HAY, Vol. II, p. 261:

"There were great losses in the elections in consequence of the Emancipation Proclamation.''

EXTRACT FROM LETTER, September 28, 1863, from Abraham Lincoln to Hannibal Hamlin:

"While I hope something from this proclamation, my expectations are not so sanguine as are those of some friends. The time for its effect southward has not come; but northward the effect should be instantneous. It is six days old and while commendation in newspapers and by distinguished individuals is all that a vain man could wish, the stocks have declined and troops come forward more slowly than ever. This looked squarely in the face is not very satisfactory. We have fewer troops in the field at the end of six days than we had at the beginning—the attrition among the old, outnumbering the addition by the new. The North responds to the proclamation sufficiently *in breath;* but breath alone kills no rebels. I wish I could write more cheerfully.''

Not a negro in the States that did not secede was freed by Lincoln's Proclamation and it had no effect even in the South as it was unconstitutional and Lincoln knew it. Many in the North resented it, and Lincoln was unhappy over the situation as Lamon testified. The negroes were freed by an amendment offered by a Southern man, John Brooks Henderson of Missouri. Emancipation did not become a law until after Lincoln's death. It is really a farce for negroes to celebrate Emancipation Day, and give Lincoln the credit.

Did Abraham Lincoln keep his pledge?

"On January 1, 1863, the second writing of the Emancipation Proclamation was read. The members of the Cabinet noticed that the name of God was not mentioned in it, and reminded the President that such an important document should recognize the name of the Deity. Lincoln said he had overlooked that fact and asked the Cabinet to assist him in preparing a paragraph recognizing God. Chief Justice Chase prepared it:

'I invoke the considerate judgment of mankind and the gracious favor of Almighty God.'

It was accepted without a change.''

SCHOULER'S "*History of the United States,*" Vol. VI., p. 21:

"People found in Lincoln before his death nothing remarkably good or great, but on the contrary found in him the reverse of goodness or greatness.

"Lincoln as one of Fame's immortals does not appear in the Lincoln of 1861."

HORACE GREELEY said (p. 274):

"I cannot trust 'honest old Abe'—he is too smart for me."

JUDGE JEREMIAH S. BLACK of Pennsylvania said (Black's "*Essays,*" p. 153):

"Of the wanton cruelties that Lincoln's administration has inflicted upon unoffending citizens, I have neither space nor skill, nor time, to paint them—since the fall of Robespierre, nothing has occurred to cast such disrepute on Republican institutions."

DON PIATT'S "*Reminiscences of Lincoln,*" p. 21:

"Had Lincoln lived could he have justified the loss of more than a million lives and the destruction of more than eight billions of dollars of property on a Constitutional basis? Of course he could not, and would not have been considered worthy of the honors heaped on him because of his martyrdom."

"I hear of Lincoln and read of him in eulogies and biographies and fail to recognize the man I knew in private life before he became President of the United States."

CHARLES FRANCIS ADAMS, the Massachusetts historian, says:

"When the Federal Constitution was adopted, in the case of final issue to whom did the average citizen owe allegiance? Was it to the Union or to his State?

"Sweeping aside all legal arguments and metaphysical disquisitions—I do not think the answer admits of doubt. Nine men out of ten in the North and ninety-nine out of a hundred in the South would have said ultimate allegiance was due the State.

"How then can we justify the acts of Lincoln's administration?

"An unconstitutional platform called for an unconstitutional policy.

"An unconstitutional policy called for an unconstitutional coercion.

"An unconstitutional coercion called for an unconstitutional war.

"An unconstitutional war called for an unconstitutional despotism.

"Authority uncontrolled and unlimited by men, by Constitution, by Supreme Court, or by law was Lincoln's war policy."

The St. Louis "*Globe-Democrat*," March 6, 1898:

"Where now is the man so rash as to even warmly criticize Abraham Lincoln?"

One adverse comment subjects one to the accusation either of prejudice or injustice.

"In seeking the truth about him, it would be most unjust to take only the testimony of his enemies, and it would be equally as unjust to take only the testimony of his glorifiers. Lincoln was a man as other men with weak points and strong points of character, and the fairest testimony ought to come from those who knew him best, loved him well, honored him and yet were friendly enough, truthful enough and just enough to see and acknowledge his faults."

In the Preface to "*The True Story of a Great Life*," written by Herndon and Weik after the first "*Life of Lincoln*," by Herndon had been destroyed is found this:

"With a view of throwing light on some attributes of Mr. Lincoln's character hitherto obscure these volumes are given to the world. The whole truth concerning Mr. Lincoln should be known. The truth will at last come out, and no man need hope to evade it. Some persons will doubtless object to the narrative of certain facts, but these facts are indispensable to a full knowledge of Mr. Lincoln. We must have all the facts about him. We must be prepared to take Mr. Lincoln as he was. Mr. Lincoln was my warm and personal friend. My purpose to tell the truth about him need occasion no apprehension. God's naked truth cannot injure his fame."

LAMON'S "*Life of Lincoln*":

"The ceremony of Mr. Lincoln's apotheosis was planned and executed after his death by men who were unfriendly to him while he lived. Men who had exhausted the resources of their skill and ingenuity in venomous detractions of the living Lincoln were the first after his death, to undertake the task of guarding his memory not as a human being, but as a god."

LAMON again says:

"There was fierce rivalry who should canonize Mr. Lincoln in the most solemn words; who should compare him

to the most sacred character in all history. He was proph-
et, priest, and king, he was Washington, he was Moses, he
was likened to Christ the Redeemer, he was likened unto
God. After that came the ceremony of apotheosis. And
this was the work of men who never spoke of the living
Lincoln except with jeers and contempt. After his death
it became a *political necessity* to *pose him as 'the greatest,
wisest, Godliest man that ever lived.'* ''

LAMON:

''Those who scorned and reviled him while living were
Secretary of the Treasury, Salmon P. Chase; Secretary of
War, Edwin Stanton; Vice-President, Hannibal Hamlin;
Secretary of State, Wm. Seward, Fremont; Senators Sum-
ner, Trumbull, Ben Wade, Henry Wilson, Thaddeus Ste-
vens, Henry Ward Beecher, Wendell Phillips, Winter
Davis, Horace Greeley, Zack Chandler of Michigan, and a
host of others.''

General Don Piatt travelled with Lincoln when he was making
his campaign speeches, hence knew him intimately.

GENERAL DON PIATT says:

''When a leader dies all good men go to lying about
him. From the moment that covers his remains to the
last echo of the rural press, in speeches, in sermonts, eulogies, reminiscences, we hear nothing but pious lies.''

GENERAL PIATT continues:

''Abraham Lincoln has almost disappeared from human
knowledge. I hear of him, I read of him in eulogies and
biographies but I fail to recognize the man I knew in life.''

GENERAL PIATT says:

''Lincoln faced and lived through the awful responsi-
bilitiy of the war with a courage that came from indifference.''

One may say the spirit of that Gettysburg address should
be emulated.

Lamon says that ''is not the speech Mr. Lincoln made at
Gettysburg.''

Nicolay says ''it was revised.''

Lamon says all that the biographers say of ''Mr. Everett's
commendatory words is bosh.''

Mr. Everett was disappointed in the speech and so was Mr.
Seward.

LAMON, in his *"Recollections of Lincoln,"* said after the speech was over Lincoln said:

"Lamon, that speech was like a wet blanket on the audience. I am distressed about it."

On the platform, Mr. Seward asked Everett, the orator of the day, what he thought of the President's speech.

MR. EVERETT replied:

"It is not what I expected. I am disappointed. What do you think of it, Mr. Seward?"

MR. SEWARD replied:

"He has made a failure."

See (on p. 173) what Lamon says occurred after his death:

" 'Amid the tears, sobs and cheers it produced in the excited throng, the orator of the day (Mr. Everett) turned to Mr. Lincoln, grasped his hand and exclaimed: 'I congratulate you on your success,' adding in a transport of heated enthusiasm, 'Mr. President, how gladly would I give my hundred pages to be the author of your twenty lines.'

"Nothing of the kind ever occurred. I state it as a fact and without fear of contradiction, that this Gettysburg speech was not regarded as a production of extraordinary merit, nor was it commented on as such *until after the death of Mr. Lincoln.*

"The fame of Lincoln concentrates its vital power upon his achievements in the sphere of oratory. Above all, does this criterion, or test, hold good of his much-vaunted Gettysburg address, delivered November 19, 1863. By one of those revealing ironies to which both literary and oratorical renown are ever subject the special phrase that has been most thoroughly ingrained and assimilated into the heart and speech of the world traces its suggestion, if not its specific origin, to Webster's memorable reply to Hayne during the historic debate of January, 1830. By reference to Webster's argument as edited by Bradley's *"Orations and Arguments* (p. 227, par. 5), the reader will discover at a glance the very essence of the language, 'government of the people, by the people, and for the people,' so intensely associated with the memory of Lincoln. Note the harmony existing between the words of Webster uttered in 1830 and those which fell from Lincoln at Gettysburg in November, 1863:

" 'It is the people's government, made for the people, made by the people, and answerable to the people.' (Bradley, p. 227, par. 5).

"The resemblance existing between the passages cited is

too minute and definite to admit of explanation as a mere
coincidence of form or a simple analogy in the mode of ex-
position. Even if we waive the charge of willful plagiar-
ism, the most exuberant charity cannot ignore or condone
the palpable and wanton imitation of the thought and dic-
tion of Daniel Webster.''

HENRY E. SHEPHERD, Baltimore, Md.:

"It is now quite well known that Mr. Lincoln did not
write the Gettysburg speech as it appears in all text books
on American Literature which have been written by Northern men, and in nearly all Readers used in Southern schools.
His intimate friend, Lamon's testimony is corroborated by
William Seward, Edward Everett, who sat on the stage
with him, and others who were present when the speech
was made. And yet Jefferson Davis the author of several
published books is omitted from the text books of American Literature written by Northern men, and Abraham
Lincoln put in because of a speech he never wrote.''

Did Lincoln write that speech accredited to him, or was it
doctored by one of his ardent admirers?

Montgomery City, Mo., *The Star:*

"It was my privilege to be present at the dedication of
the Soldiers' National Cemetery at Gettysburg the afternoon of November 19, 1863, and to hear the now famous
address of Abraham Lincoln on that occasion. I can bear
witness to the fact that this address, pronounced by Edward
Everett to be unequalled in the annals of oratory, fell upon
unappreciative ears, was entirely unnoticed and wholly
disappointing to a majority of the hearers. This may have
been owing in part to the careless and undemonstrative
delivery of the orator, but the fact is that he had concluded
his address and resumed his seat before most of the audience realized that he had begun to speak. It was my good
fortune as a newspaper correspondent to occupy a place
directly beside Mr. Lincoln when he delivered this brief
oration and on the other side of the speaker was W. H.
Seward. Other members of the Cabinet had seats on the
stand and I also noticed Governor Curtin, Seymour, Tod,
Morton and Bradford; Edward Everett and Col. John
W. Forney.

"At the conclusion of Mr. Everett's scholarly oration,
Mr. Lincoln faced the vast audience. He looked haggard
and pale and wore a shabby overcoat, from an inside pocket of which he drew a small roll of manuscript. He read
his address in a sort of drawling monotone, the audience remaining perfectly silent. The few pages were soon fin-

ished. Mr. Lincoln doubled up his manuscript, thrust it back into his overcoat pocket and sat down—not a word, not a cheer, not a shout. The people looked at one another, seeming to say, 'Is that all?'

"I am well aware that accounts have differed as to the manner of this address and its reception 'by the audience. I was an eye witness and hearer and my position was immediately beside the speaker, therefore the foregoing account may be relied upon." (W. H. Cunningham, Reporter for *The Star*, Montgomery City, Mo.)

HISTORY before his martyrdom said:

"Lincoln detested science and literature. No man can put his finger on any book written in the last or present century that Lincoln read through. He read little." (Herndon).

HERNDON, in his *"Story of a Great Life,"* says on page 47:

"When Abe saw that Grisby was getting the best of the fight, he burst through the ring, caught Grisby, threw him some feet distant; then stood up, proud as Lucifer, swinging a bottle of liquor over his head and swearing aloud, 'I am the big buck of the lick! If anybody doubts it let him come and whet his horns.' "

Lamon in his *"Life of Lincoln,"* tells the same story only adds that Grisby challenged him to shoot with pistols, but Lincoln replied: "I am not going to fool away my life on a single shot."

Lincoln should not be held up as an example for Christian children.

HERNDON's letter to Lamon:

"In New Salem Mr. Lincoln lived with a class of men, moved with them, had his being with them. They were scoffers of religion, made loud protests against the followers of Christianity. They denied that Jesus Christ was the Son of God. They ridiculed old divines, and made them skeptics by their logic. In 1835 Mr. Lincoln wrote a book on infidelity and intended to have it published but Hill, believing that if the book should be published it would kill Lincoln as a politician, threw it into a stove and it went up in smoke and ashes before Lincoln could seize it.

"When Mr. Lincoln became a candidate for the Legislature he was accused of being an infidel and he never denied it. He was accused of saying Jesus was not the Son of God, and he never denied it.

"In 1854 he made me erase the name of God from a speech

1 was about to make. He did this also to one of his friends in Washington City.

"I know when he left Springfield for Washington he had undergone no change in his opinion on religion."

DENNIS HANKS, Lincoln's first cousin, says:

"Abe would often collect a crowd of boys and men around him to make fun of the preacher. He frequently reproduced the sermon with a nasal twang, rolling his eyes, and all sorts of droll aggravations, to the great delight of the wild fellows assembled. Sometimes he broke out with stories passably humorous and invariably vulgar."

MR. JESSE E. FALL, one of Lincoln's intimate friends, says:

"Mr. Lincoln's friends were not a little surprised at finding in his biographies statements of his religious opinions utterly at variance with his known sentiments."

Again HERNDON says:

"His stepmother denied that he ever went into a corner to 'ponder sacred writings and wet the pages with his tears of penitence."

LAMON, in his "Life of Lincoln," says:

"When he went to New Salem he consorted with free thinkers, and joined them in deriding the gospel story of Jesus. He wrote a labored book on this subject, which his friend Hill burned up. Not until after Mr. Lincoln's death were any of these facts denied."

DENNIS HANKS says:

"Abe did not sing sacred songs, but the songs he sang were of a very questionable character."

On page 63 of LAMON'S "Life of Lincoln" is found:

"Abe wrote many satires which are only remembered in fragments; if we had them in full they would be too indecent to print."

If Abraham Lincoln had believed that God's Word is inspired, and had believed in the Divinity of our Lord, and had ever connected himself with a Christian church then he could be held up as a model, possibly, for Christian children to emulate. But as he failed in all these essentials for a Christian's belief and practice it is dangerous to have our young people have him held up as an exemplar.

They would feel it is not necessary to believe in God's Word; it is not necessary to believe that Jesus Christ is the Son of God; it is not necessary to publicly confess Him before men.

They would naturally think if "the greatest man that ever lived in the world" did not find these things necessary, why should they?

Holland's *"Life of Lincoln"* is a *"Pretended Life of Lincoln,"* written after his apotheosis begun.

Ida Tarbell's *"Life of Lincoln"* was called by Herndon and Lamon a *"So-called Life of Lincoln."*

It will not be safe for ministers of the gospel, editors of Christian newspapers, Sunday School teachers, public speakers or true historians to quote from those who deified Lincoln after martyrdom.

PART II.

Abraham Lincoln As He Was Not—(After His Assassination).

AUTHORITY:

Northern writers claim that Abraham Lincoln was "the greatest man that ever lived;" that he was "the Godliest man that has walked the earth since Christ."

ALBERT BUSHNELL HART:

"Abraham Lincoln was the greatest man of the Civil War Period."

SUNDAY SCHOOL TIMES:

"Abraham Lincoln is the Christian exemplar for children today."

JUDD STEWART, Address, North Plainfield, N. J., Feb. 10, 1917:

"Here in this new world country with no pride of ancestry arose the greatest man since the meek and lowly Nazarene; a man whose life had a greater influence on the human race than any teacher, thinker or toiler since the beginning of the Christian Era."

P. D. Ross, an Englishman, in *"Harper's Weekly,"* November 7, 1908, said:

"Abraham Lincoln is the greatest man that the world has ever possessed."

DON PIATT, after Lincoln's martyrdom, says:

"The greatest figure looming up in our history."

Stanton, before his death, in a letter to President Buchanan, expressed his contempt for Lincoln. He also advised the revolutionary overthrow of the Lincoln government in order that McClellan be made military dictator.

After his assassination, standing over Lincoln's dead body, he said, "Now he belongs to the ages."

JOHN HAY, *Secretary* of State, said (after Lincoln's death) :

"Abraham Lincoln, First President of the Republican party, the greatest, wisest, Godliest man that has appeared on earth since Christ."

J. G. HOLLAND :

"Lincoln unequalled since Washington in services to the Nation." ·

J. G. HOLLAND waited until after Lincoln died to say :

"Mr. Lincoln will always be remembered as eminently a Christian President. Conscience, not popular applause, not love of power, was the ruling motive of Lincoln's life. No stimulant ever entered his mouth, no profanity ever came from his lips."

J. G. HOLLAND :

"Abraham Lincoln was the first of all men who have walked the earth since the Nazarene."

WILLIAM M. DAVIDSON :

"Abraham Lincoln was the greatest statesmen of the Nineteenth Century."

J. B. WADE :

"History will show Abraham Lincoln to be the greatest man that ever lived."

J. M. MERRILL, in *Detroit Free Press*, says :

"Abraham Lincoln is so far above every other man in human history that to compare him to others seems sac-sacrilege.

"No where on the earth is there a historic character to compare to our sainted martyr, Abraham Lincoln."

If this adulation of him was taken from what was said of him *before his martyrdom* the South would be willing to accept it— but the South is not willing to accept what has been said of him since that period, for it does not tally with his life as given by his friends and those who knew him best. Herndon, his friend and law partner for twenty years; Lamon, an intimate friend and one who often acted as private secretary to him; his step-mother, whom he idolized; Dennis Hanks, his cousin and playmate—all of these loved him, but were honest, saw his faults and were willing to acknowledge them.

Testimony such as: John Hay, his Secretary of State, Nicolay, a personal friend, Ida Tarbell and J. G. Holland, who put him on a pedestal, worshipped him and were blind to his faults, should not be held as reliable.

WALTER McELREATH, after. reading Rothschild's *"Lincoln: Master of Men"*:

"Mr. Lincoln was not an ordinary man we all agree, but greatness is a relative term and considering the opportunities and responsibilities and station which Mr. Lincoln occupied he must be judged by the standards of greatness by which other great men are judged. Judging him by these standards I cannot see how Mr. Lincoln was at all a great man or how he can be said to possess even the second order of greatness.

"How can a man be considered great when the men associated with him four years in such an enterprise as civil war were not impressed with his greatness until the enterprise was over, is more than I can understand.

"McClellan had known him years before the war and was not impressed with his greatness. Chase, Seward and Stanton never thought him a great man until after his death. It is strange that such men living close to him for four years could not recognize in him some signs of greatness while he lived. I cannot see anything great in his choice of men or generals. His ministers were chosen to remove them from opposition to the administration. He held the power to depose—his mastery over men came from his power to exercise unlimited authority."

JAS. A. STEVENS:

"Mr. Lincoln was a great man and a patriot, yet there is no doubt his cruel taking off had not a little to do with his exaltation to the position he now occupies in the eyes of a sympathetic world."

DR. LITTLEFIELD, Needham, Mass.:

"Lee's shrine at Lexington, not Lincoln's tomb. will be the shrine of American patriotism when once history is told correctly."

XV.

Reconstruction Was Not Just to the South. This Injustice Made the Ku Klux Klan a Necessity.

AUTHORITY:

RIDPATH'S *"Universal History,"* p. 176:

"It was soon seen, however, by Congress and the North,

to follow the method suggested by President Johnson would be to remand at once the control of the lately seceded States into the hand of the old Confederate party. *Right* or *wrong,* it was determined that this should not be done, and Congress determined that the military and suppressive method of governing the seceded States should be employed." .

MUZZEY's *"American History,"* p. 486:

"The rules of these negro governments of 1868 was an indescribable orgy of extravagance, fraud and disgusting incompetence—a travesty on government. Unprincipled politicians dominated the States' government and plunged the States further and further into debt by voting themselves enormous salaries, and reaping in many ways hundreds of thousands of dollars in graft. In South Carolina $200,000 were spent in furnishing the State Capitol with costly plate glass mirrors, lounges, arm chairs, a free bar and other luxurious appointments for the use of the negro and scalawag legislators. It took the South nine years to get rid of these governments."

MARK TWAIN said:

"The eight years in America, 1860-1868, uprooted institutions centuries old, and wrought so profoundly upon the national character of the people that its influence will be felt for two or three generations."

"Secret Political Societies in the South,," by Walter Henry Cook, Cleveland, Ohio, Western Reserve University:

"A new economic system could have been built up by the men and women of the South with freed slaves had they been left alone. The policy of Thad Stevens and Charles Sumner after Lincoln's death stirred up ex-slaves to hate the white men of the South, especially when they preached a gospel of social equality for which the men of the South would not stand under any circumstances."

The next quotation is from Dan Vorhees, Representative for many years, and later a United States Senator from Indiana. In his speech, *"Plunder of Eleven States,"* made in the House of Representatives, March 23, 1872, he pictures well the animus of Reconstruction. He said:

"From turret to foundation you tore down the government of eleven States. You left not one stone upon another. You not only destroyed their local laws, but you trampled upon their ruins. You called conventions to frame new Constitutions for these old States. You not only said who should be elected to rule over these States, but you said

who should elect them. You fixed the quality and the color
of the voters. You purged the ballot box' of intelligence
and virtue, and in their stead you placed the most ignorant
and unqualified race in the world to rule over these people."

Then taking State by State he showed what Thad Stevens'
policy had done:

."Let the great State of Georgia speak first," he said.
"You permitted her to stand up and start in her new career, but seeing some flaw in your handiwork, you again
destroyed and again reconstructed her State government.
You clung to her throat; you battered her features out of
shape and recognition, determined that your party should
have undisputed possession and enjoyment of her offices,
her honors, and her substance. Then bound hand and foot
you handed her over to the rapacity of robbers. Her pro-
lific and unbounded resources inflamed their desires.

"In 1861 Georgia was free from debt. Taxes were light
as air. The burdens of government were easy upon her
citizens. Her credit stood high, and when the war closed
she was still free from indebtedness. After six years of
Republican rule you present her, to the horror of the world,
loaded with a debt of $50,000,000, and the crime against
Georgia is the crime this same party has committed against
the other Southern States. Your work of destruction was
more fatal than a scourge of pestilence, war or famine.

"Rufus B. Bullock, Governor of Georgia, dictated the
legislation of Congress, and the great commonwealth of
Georgia was cursed by his presence. With such a Governor, and such a legislature in perfect harmony, morally
and politically, their career will go down to posterity without a rival for infamous administrations of the world. That
Governor served three years and then absconded with all
of the gains. The Legislature of two years spent $100,000
more than had been spent during any eight previous years.
They even put the children's money, laid aside for education of white and black, into their own pockets."

When Senator Voorhees came to South Carolina, the proud
land of Marion and Sumter, his indignation seems to have
reached its pinnacle:

"There is no form of ruin to which she has not fallen a
prey, no curse with which she has not been baptized, no cup
of humiliation and suffering her people have not drained
to the dregs. There she stands the result of your handiwork, bankrupt in money, ruined in credit, her bonds
hawked about the streets at ten cents on the dollar, her

prosperity blighted at home and abroad, without peace, happiness, or hope. There she stands with her skeleton frame admonishing all the world of the loathsome consequences of a government fashioned in hate and fanaticism, and founded upon the ignorant and vicious classes of manhood. Her sins may have been many and deep, and the color of scarlet, yet they will become as white as snow in comparison with those you have committed against her in the hour of her helplessness and distress.''

Then he took up in like manner State after State, and wound up with this:

"I challenge the darkest annals of the human race for a parallel to the robberies which have been perpetrated on these eleven American States. Had you sown seeds of kindness and good will they would long ere this have blossomed into prosperity and peace. Had you sown seeds of honor, you would have reaped a golden harvest of contentment and obedience. Had you extended your charities and your justice to a distressed people you would have awakened a grateful affection in return. But as you planted in hate and nurtured in corruption so have been the fruits which you have gathered.''

Quoting again from Walter Henry Cook in regard to Reconstruction graft:

"Governor Warmouth of Louisiana accumulated one and a half million in four years on a salary of $8,000 a year. Governor Moses of South Carolina acknowledged that he had accepted $65,000 in bribes. Governor Clayton of Arkansas said he intended to people the State with negroes. The carpetbag government of Florida stole meat and flour given for helpless women and children. In North Carolina and Alabama negro convicts were made justices of the peace, men who were unable to read or write. In the South Carolina Legislature 94 black men were members. The Speaker of the House, the Clerk of the House, the doorkeeper, the chairman of the Ways and Means Committee, and the Chaplain, were all black men and some of them could neither read nor write.''

The next is an extract from *The Chicago Chronicle,* written by a Northern man:

"The Fifteenth Amendment to the Constitution grew out of a spirit of revenge, for the purpose of punishing the Southern people. It became a part of the Constitution by fraud and force to secure the results of war. The war was not fought to secure negro suffrage.

"The history of the world may be searched in vain for a parallel to the spirit of savagery which it inflicted upon a defeated and impoverished people, the unspeakable barbarous rule of a servile race just liberated from bondage. Negro suffrage was a crime against the white people of the South. It was a crime against the blacks of the South. It was a crime against the whole citizenship of the Republic. Political power was never conferred upon a race so poorly equipped to receive it."

Now a last quotation from Charles Francis Adams, the grandson of John Quincy Adams:

"I have ever been one of those who have thought extremely severe measures were dealt the Southern people after the Civil War, measures of unprecedented severity. The Southern community was not only desolated during the war but $3,000,000,000 of property confiscated after the war. I am not aware that history records a similar act super-added to the destruction and desolation of war."

Again:

"Their manumitted slaves belonging to an inferior and alien race, were enfranchised and put in control of the whole administration. Is there a similar case recorded in history? If so I have never heard of it. It was simply a case of insane procedure, and naturally resulted in disaster. We stabbed the South to the quick, and during all the years of Reconstruction turned the dagger round and round in the festering wound. If the South had been permitted to secede, slavery would have died a natural death."

The United States government is the only government that ever freed her slaves without giving just compensation for them.

Dr. Wyeth in his *"With Sabre and Scalpel,"* published by Harper & Brothers, New York, says:

"None but those who went through this period have any conception of it. Defeat on battlefield brought no dishonor, but all manner of oppressions, with poverty and enforced domination of a race lately in slavery brought humiliation and required a courage little less than superhuman."

Abraham Lincoln advocated paying the South for her slaves·

"The slaves taken from the South by arms should be paid for."

Lincoln was right. God has never allowed a nation to prosper where a known wrong is kept unrighted.

"Secret Political Societies in the South During the Period of

Reconstruction," Walter Henry Cook; Western Reserve University, Cleveland, Ohio:

"The Ku Klux accomplished much. From a poliitcal viewpoint it secured home rule for several of the Southern States; it ended the disgraceful rule of the carpetbaggers therein; and it helped to re-establish honest and efficient governmental institutions. This example was an inspiration which after 1872 soon led the men of the Southern States still in Radical control to a *glorious victory* in regaining self-government. From an economic standpoint, the negroes had been frightened into going to work, and were prevented, to a large extent, from breaking labor contracts. These were important services in the rehabilitation of the South. From a social standpoint the Klan had protected property, had protected life, and had brought order out of chaos."

MRS. ROSE'S "History of the Ku Klux Klan," Historian-General, U. D. C.:

"The Ku Klux were opposed to the shedding of human blood, and violence was never used except as a last resort. Repeated warnings were given to offenders, and it was only when they were not heeded that the Ku Klux resorted to extreme measures.

"The methods of the Ku Klux Klan were generally peaceful and without destruction of life and property, and when its objects had been accomplished there was no persecution, nor pillaging, nor hounding of any one—and when tranquility was restored to the land, the Ku Klux folded their tents like the Arabs, and as silently stole away."

XVI.

Race Prejudice Is Stronger in the North Than in the South.

Before the Sixties, lynchings of negroes in the South were of very rare occurrence—there was no occasion for it—we had no incendiary literature distributed among the negroes until John Brown tried it and failed. The incendiary literature is now largely responsible for present day conditions.

The South is the negro's friend. The South wants the negro to stay in the South. The South has not encouraged immigration from the Latin States for fear of race antagonism. All that the South asks is to be let alone in her management of the negro, so that the friendly relations may continue.

The Southern people encourage the negroes to buy land and have their own homes. The climate of the South suits the negro best—the South is his logical home.

The South claims that race prejudice has been, and now is, far greater in the North than in the South.

In his *"Democracy in America,"* De Tocqueville, the French writer, says:

"Though the electoral franchise has been conferred on the negroes in all the free States, if they come forward to vote their lives are in danger. Negroes may serve by law on juries but prejudice repels them from office. They have separate schools, separate hospital wards, and separate galleries in the theatres. In the South it is quite different with the negro. Undoubtedly, the prejudice of the race appears to be stronger in the States that have abolished slaves than in the States where slavery still exists.

"White carpenters, white bricklayers and white painters will not work side by side with the blacks in the North but do it in almost every Southern State unless Northern men among their workmen oppose it. But in the South white men do not sit down to eat with black men as they do in many parts of the North."

Negroes left their homes in Alabama to work in Illinois, but many were killed and others driven from the State. Were the murderers of those negroes ever brought to trial?

One Republican said:

"If any more negroes come to Illinois, I will meet them on the border with gatling-guns!"

Mr. Seward, March 3, 1858, said:

"The white man needs this continent to labor in and must have it."

The Legislature of Kansas, the home of John Brown, said:

"This State is for whites only."

In 1850, 1855 and 1865, Michigan refused suffrage to free negroes.

In 1864 no negro could vote in Nevada.

"In Illinois (Lincoln's State) no negro nor mulatto was allowed to remain in the State ten days.

"If a negro came into the State he was to be sold at auction."

In twenty-seven counties of Indiana no negro was allowed to

live. If any white man encouraged him to come to the State he was fined.

In Boston the negroes are segregated.

In Ohio the negroes were warned if they did not segregate some dire calamity would befall them.

In New York City and Washington City this question of segregation is of serious import today and under constant discussion.

No negro can live in Oregon.

MUZZEY's "*American History*":

> "Ohio, in 1867, at the very time that Congress was forcing negro suffrage on the South, rejected by 50,000 votes to give the ballot to the few negroes in that State."

LUNT's "*Origin of the Late War*":

> "The negroes were perfectly happy in their condition of slavery in the South—they were not only happy but proud of it. They labored it is true for their daily bread, but they were nursed in sickness, and cared for in old age. Upon certain conditions they could obtain freedom. Freedom was frequently granted for faithful services."

The South never understood why the abolitionists made a bitter fight against slavery under humane Christian masters in the South and no fight at all against the slave trade in the North. If cruelty to Africans was really their object in fighting slavery, the slave ships where they were huddled together standing during the long voyage offered the best objects of attack.

As to the condition of the slaves in the South under the institution of slavery, Major-General Quitman, of New York, an army officer who was stationed near a Mississippi plantation before the war, says in a letter to his father:

> "'Every night she has family prayers with her slaves. When a minister comes, which is very frequently, prayers are said night and morning, and chairs are always provided for the servants.
>
> "They are married by a clergyman of their own color, and a sumptuous supper is always prepared. They are a happy, careless, unreflecting, good-natured race—who left to themselves would degenerate into drones or brutes. They have great family pride and are the most arrant aristocrats in the world." ("*The Secession War in America*," by J. P. Shaffull, published in New York, 1862).

"Are the white slaves today—those in the industrial bondage—as well cared for as were the black slaves before the civil war? Is the industrial slave as well fed, as well clothed, as well housed as these slaves were by their masters?

"Are the industrial slaves that work in the mills and mines and sweat shops of today as well cared for as were the slaves of the South that worked in the fields?" (Copied from an editorial in Pittsburg (Pa.) Daily).

It was suggested that the negroes be put into the Confederate army with a promise of freedom when the war ended. The North felt assured that the negroes would never fight for the South.

Dr. Hancock, in the Richmond Hospital, put them to the test. Out of seventy-two approached on the subject sixty said:

"Yes, they would gladly go to protect their master's families and would fight the enemy to the bitter end." ("*War of Rebellion*" Series IV., Vol. II., p. 1193).

"*Boston Herald,*" September 12, 1919:

"Feeling against William Lloyd Garrison and other abolitionists ran high in this city in 1851, but it was in New York that the home of a prominent citizen was sacked, it was in Philadelphia that a public hall was burned by a mob in the presence of the mayor and the police.

"Harrison Gray Otis, in Faneuil Hall, denounced the English anti-slavery orator, George Thompson, as hired by British gold to destroy the Union.

"At a gathering in the building that housed 'The Liberator,' a mob caught Garrison, tied a rope about his neck to drag him through the streets.

"A body of colored men at another time took Shadrack, the colored waiter at the Coffee House from the officers of the law, and sent him away to Canada.

"When Thomas Sims was sent back to slavery the Court House was surrounded with breast-high chains by the United States Marshal, so that the judges, and all others having business in the building were obliged to stoop in order to reach the doors, and that day seems mild to the mobs in Boston today."

XVII.

The South Was More Interested in the Freedom of the Slaves Than the North.

In 1816, *"The African Colonization Society"* was organized with James Madison, a slaveholder, as president. Thomas Jefferson, a slaveholder, testifies that slaveholders were planning to free their slaves.

When James Monroe became President he secured a tract of land about the size of Mississippi on the West coast of Africa, named Liberia, and its capital was called Monrovia to honor him, and to this the slaves as freed were to be sent. In 1847 it became a Republic with only negroes as officers. Then it was protected from many encroachments of European monarchies by the Monroe Doctrine. It was Southern statesmen and slaveholders who were most interested in this, although Northern philanthropists greatly aided by moral and material support.

Charles Francis Adams, Jr., the historian, realized this and said:

"Had the South been allowed to manage this question unfettered the slaves would have been—ere this—fully emancipated and that without bloodshed or race problems."

Again, the fact stands that Thomas Jefferson, a large slaveholder, when Virginia ceded her Northwest Territory, made it a condition that slavery should not be allowed in it, and no one from the South objected.

A committee of five Virginians—Jefferson, Pendleton, Wythe, Mason and Thomas Lee—was appointed to revise the laws and prepare all slaveholders in the State for the gradual emancipation of their slaves. This law said:

"All children born after the passage of the Act should be free, but must remain with their mothers until old enough to be self-supporting."

Thirty-two times Virginia legislated against slavery.

Thomas Jefferson urged that all slaveholders free their slaves by gradual emancipation as soon as possible, for by the Missouri Compromise, where a State's right was interfered with by other States, he saw plainly that the day might come when sudden emancipation would take place, and he said "human nature shudders at the prospect of it," but he thanked God he would not be alive to see it.

George Washington urged the gradual emancipation of his slaves and freed them by his will, and told Thomas Jefferson he wished all slaves could be freed.

George Mason believed in emancipation of his slaves and freed them.

John Randolph, of Roanoke, freed his slaves and bought territory in Ohio to place them.

Henry Clay urged the gradual emancipation of the slaves.

General Lee and his mother believed in gradual emancipation, and practiced it and so did many slaveholders at the South. Hundreds of thousands of slaves had been freed in the South before 1820.

CONGRESSIONAL RECORDS:

"Jefferson Davis when in the United States Senate, urged that a plan be made for emancipation that would be best for the slaveholders and the slave. This was why Southern men were so insistent about securing more slave territory to relieve the congested condition of the slave States that they might prepare the slaves as freed for their future government."

ABRAHAM LINCOLN said:

"Gradual emancipation was the best plan, and the North should not criticize too severely the Southern brethren for tardiness in this matter."

"The Abolition Crusade which began at the time of the Missouri Compromise in 1820, and which reached an intense pitch in 1839, caused Southern men to withdraw membership in abolition societies."

The South claims Northern slaveholders were more anxious to hold their slaves than were the slaveholders of the South.

"In 1860 there were only 3,950,531 slaves in the South and many wills had been written freeing them by gradual emancipation. Many of the slaves in the South before the war belonged to Northern slaveholders. Girard, of Philadelphia, worked his slaves on a large sugar plantation in Louisiana. It was from the profits of this plantation Girard College was built. Hemmingway, of Boston, had his slaves on a plantation—not in the Southern States, but in Cuba—and his will left them to his daughter as late as 1870."

RICHARDSON'S "Defense of the South," p. 20:

"Thomas Elkins, of Effingham County, Georgia, before 1860, offered to free his slaves and send them back to

Africa at his own expense and the slaves begged to let them remain with him. Among these slaves were the sons of African kings and princes.''

LUNDY'S *"Universal Emancipation":*

"There were before the Missouri Compromise, 1820, 106 anti-slavery societies—with 5,150 members in the South, and 24 abolition societies in the North with only 920 members.''

In 1831, Virginia wanted a bill passed for gradual emancipation of the slaves and it was lost by *one* vote—that of the chairman. Virginia made 23 attempts to legislate about freeing the slaves and abolishing the slave trade. When 61 women and children were murdered by Nat Turner's insurrection at Southhampton, Va., the abolition societies in the South disbanded.

The only colony to forbid slaves was Georgia.

The first State to legislate against the slave trade was Georgia.

The first bill to allow a slaveholder to free his slaves was offered by Thomas Jefferson, of Virginia.

Thomas Jefferson, of Virginia, urged in the Declaration of Independence that the slave trade be forbidden. John Adams, of Massachusetts, urged that clause be omitted.

The only State that made it a felony to buy a slave was Virginia.

Thomas Jefferson insisted that Ohio, Illinois, Indiana, Michigan, and Wisconsin should not be slave states—and yet Virginia, a slave State, gave this territory.

A committee was appointed to draw up these resolutions to present to the Massachusetts Legislature when sectional feeling was at its height. They calmly and deliberately weighed the arguments on the side of slaveholders, and then as calmly and deliberately weighed those on the side of the abolitionists. Then they came to a conclusion—they said:

"Nothing which is not founded upon the eternal principles of truth and justice can ever long prevail against an irresistible force of public disapprobation. Your committee feel that the conduct of the abolitionists is not only wrong in policy but erroneous in morals.

"Your committee are determined to fulfill their duty to the State and to our common country in the most firm and faithful manner. In remembering that while they are men of Massachusetts, they are incapable of meanly forgetting that they also are Americans.'' (George Lunt, Chairman).

In *"The Sectional Controversy,"* (published in 1864 when the author, W. C. Fowler, was a member of the Connecticut Legislature) the author says that fifteen or twenty years earlier, when a prominent member of Congress who afterward became a member of a Presidential Cabinet was coming out from a heated sectional debate, he was asked by the writer, an old college friend:

"Will you tell me what is the real reason why Northern men encourage those petitions (for the abolition of slavery)?"

The reply was:

"The real reason is that the South will not let us have a tariff, and we touch them where they will feel it."

In this same work Mr. Fowler repeats a statement made in 1859 by Salmon P. Chase, a native of New England, who was then the Governor of Ohio, and after serving in Lincoln's Cabinet was appointed Chief Justice of the Supreme Court. Talking to W. D. Chadwick Glover, he said:

"I do not wish to have the slave emancipated because I love *him,* but because I hate his master."

"When John Brown came into Virginia to 'free the slaves by the authority of God Almighty,' Governor John A. Andrews, of Massachusetts, was one of his chief supporters, the hope of the Massachusetts abolitionists being that the appearance of Brown and his little band would excite the slaves to rise up and murder the white people. But in September, 1862, when General Dix proposed to remove a number of escaped slaves from Fortress Monroe to Massachusetts, this Governor objected, saying: 'I do not concur in any way or to any degree to the plan proposed. Permit me to say that the Northern States are of all places the worst possible to select for an asylum for negroes."

In Rice's *"Reminiscences of Abraham Lincoln,"* General Don Piatt who canvassed a part of Illinois for Mr. Lincoln in 1860 and spent some time in the company of the President-elect, says:

"He knew and saw clearly that the free States had not only no sympathy with the abolition of slavery but held fanatics, as abolitionists were called, in utter abhorrence."

And in another place he says:

"Descended from the poor whites of a slave State through many generations, Lincoln inherited the contempt, if not the hatred, held by that class for the negro. . . . . And he could no more feel a sympathy for that wretched race than he could for the horse he worked or the hog he killed."

And to all this it is interesting to add the views of John Sherman, the brother of the famous William Tecumseh. On April 2, 1862, he said in the Senate:

"We do not like the negroes. We do not disguise our dislike. As my friend from Indiana (Mr. Wright) said yesterday: 'The whole people of the Northwestern States are opposed to having many negroes among them and that principle or prejudice has been engraved in the legislation fo nearly all of the Northwestern States.' "

And let it not be forgotten that the Northwestern States at that time were inhabited mainly by people who had emigrated, or those whose ancestors had emigrated, from Northern States, most of them perhaps from New England.

It may be difficult, therefore, for honest seekers after truth to understand what Northern writers mean by "the moral awakening of the North" and the "dictatorial policy of the South."

Slavery would not have continued in the South had the Confederacy succeeded. The supremacy of the white man would have been preserved and the distinction of the races maintained.

Thomas Jefferson called the slave trade "Piratical warfare, the opprobium of infidel powers," "a calamity of most alarming nature."

The House of Burgesses in Virginia resolved to purchase no slaves that had not been in the country twelve months. under a penalty of $5,000 to the one who sold a slave and $2,500 for the buyer of a slave. This was to discourage the slave trade.

Did Massachusetts and other New England or Eastern States free their slaves or sell them?

The chief cause of race riots today is the incendiary newspapers published by the negroes in Chicago, New York, Omaha, Washington City and other places. Suppress these newspapers and arrest the editors and race riots will cease. The South knows the negro better than the North and better than the negro, born free, and raised in the North.

When such abuse comes from the North about lynching and crimes in the South, is it not radically unfair to bring the charges upon violation of mob law in Georgia—and I am not defending mob law, *I think it awful wherever found*—when they never seem to realize that the home of mob law was in New England and other Northern States?

Was not Garrison dragged by a mob in the streets of Boston? Did not New Englanders mob officers of the National government for trying to enforce the law? This was never heard of in the South.

Was not Lovejoy put to death by a mob in Illinois?

Did not the New Yorkers massacre men, women and children and burn nineteen negroes?

Was not Philadelphia the home of mobs at one time?

The Fugitive Slave Law was nullified when in 1851 a negro, Shadrack, was rescued from a United States Marshal by a mob in Boston, consisting of some of the very best citizens.

Did not a mob burn an orphanage in Philadelphia and kill women and children?

Was not a negro chained and burned at Wilmington, Delaware?

Was not a negro hanged by a mob before the court-house door at Urbana, Ohio?

Did not a mob with dynamite bombs defy the police in Chicago and not one offender brought to justice? This never happened in the South.

Will those newspapers so unjust to Georgia, and to the South as a whole, look into those mobs at Akron and Springfield, Ohio; Danville and Springfield, Illinois; Evansville and Rockport, Indiana; and Coatsville, Pennsylvania, and in States much nearer to them than Georgia? Will they not inquire into statistics and truthfully find out, if they are honest enough to admit it, that there have been more mobs proportionately to negro population in the North than in the South?

Freedom of Slaves.

GEORGE LUNT:

"We have taken counsel of our fears and have imposed upon ourselves another burden, likely to prove intolerable in the end, by the enforced discharge from restraint 3,000,-000 or 4,000,000 helpless, irresponsible creatures, hitherto entirely dependent upon others and incapable by nature, of the independent action demanded by a civilized community.

"If, then, we should now complete this notable work by conferring upon these negroes a nominal equality, and ask them to enter upon the exercise of privileges and powers to which they are and must remain forever incompetent, we shall show ourselves also most unworthy and incapable of self-government of the understanding, and not of passion or sentiment.''

GEORGE LUNT:

"However general was the dislike of slavery in the free States, yet the abolitionists proper had only here and there a local society consisting of a handful of zealous, but wrong-headed men and women of the class more recently known as strong-minded. They met in obscure apartments, and attracted scarcely any public attention; or if brought to notice by accident, were the objects of only popular ridicule and contempt. The general public mind was entirely settled in regard to the uselessness, as well as the unlawfulness of interference with slavery in the States, hence no mode of action was left to the abolitionists, except by occasional memorials to Congress upon indirect points affecting the question, or through their few unregarded publications which were read by nobody but themselves.''

GEORGE LUNT, Appendix, p. 31:

"Later, Mr. Garrison, a leader among the abolitionists, was let down by a back window, and attempted to conceal himself, but was hunted down by a mob, rescued from the hands of officers of the law and placed in the common prison. He said, 'Never before was a man so glad to get into a jail.' ''

GEORGE LUNT says (pp. 328, 330):

"So intense was the feeling on the part of such abolitionists as John Brown, that one of them actually presented in the House of Representatives a plan 'to teach the slaves to burn their masters' buildings, to kill all of their cattle, and hogs, and to conceal all farming utensils and abandon labor in seedtime and harvest so that all crops should perish,' and he goes on to say, 'such open and armed aggression on the part of John Brown betokened predetermined enmity in one part of the Union against another part; an overt act of hostility towards the government, in the peace of which only could the Union stand secure, and it was undoubtedly the signal and forerunner of war.' ''

The picture of John Brown on the way to execution, now hanging on the walls of the Metropolitan Art Gallery in New York, representing a negro woman holding her baby to be kissed by him is false to history. The physician attending him testified there was not a negro to be seen on the streets of Harper's Ferry that day.

BARNES' *"Popular History,"* p. 478:

> "On the way to the gallows, he stopped to kiss a little slave child."

The John Brown Raid and his attempt to rouse the negroes of the South to murder, insurrection and arson was punished by the death of John Brown and his accomplices by the State of Virginia and Congress said not a word, and the testimony of sane men at the North condemned the fanaticism of the insane. The South felt that the North was encouraging an interference with their slave affairs.

EDWARD EVERETT, in Fanueil Hall, said:

> "John Brown's Raid was designed to let loose the hell hounds of a servile insurrection, and to bring on a struggle which for magnitude, atrocity and horror, would have stood alone in the history of the world."

JUDGE BLACK, of Pennsylvania, said:

> "The abolitionists applauded John Brown to the echo for a series of the basest murders on record."

The South never could understand how Emerson should say of one they regarded as a horse thief, a murderer, an advocate of insurrection, that his body was "as glorious as the Cross of Christ."

ALBERT BUSHNELL HART:

> "His courage impressed even his jailers; and the abolitionists and many others saw something heroic in a man thus risking his life for the lowly."

Call Brown An Assassin.

Kansas Legislators Bitterly Assailed Osawatomie Man.

"Topeka, March 4.—J. W. Brown, representative from Butler County, set the Kansas House by the ears today by an attack on John Brown, when the bill appropriating $2,800 to preserve the John Brown cabin at Osawatomie and keep up the park surrounding it came up for passage.

"The bill was passed by the Senate several days ago and was up for final passage in the House. The bill was passed by a good vote, the Democrats generally voting against it. When Brown, who is a Democrat, was called, he voted 'no' and offered the following explanation of his vote:

" 'If John Brown had consummated his insurrection started at Harper's Ferry I probably would have died in. my youth. John Brown was never in a proper sense a resident of Kansas, nor was he 'Osawatomie Brown.' That appellation in early years having been applied to O. C. Brown, who founded the town of Osawatomie and gave it its name. He never engaged in any legitimate business or employment while here, nor did he aid any way in the improvement or development of the country. With the instincts of an anarchist and the hand of an assassin, his career in Kansas was one of lawlessness and crime—the one indelible blot on the otherwise fair free State record. No Kansan desires to appropriate money to perpetuate the name of a Booth, a Guiteau or a Czolgosz. Neither will I consent to exalt the name of the first anarchist and rebel this country produced.' "

J. J. Veath, of Washington County, a Republican, also took a slap at the Kansas hero. He voted against the bill and offered the following explanation of his vote:

"I am a Republican and I was a soldier for four years in the Union Army. I admire a brave man who with sword in hand will lead his men through shot and shell to the cannon's mouth but I despise a sneak and a bushwhacker.

"John Brown allowed his men to sharpen their swords and kill five unarmed men by cutting them to pieces in the presence of their wives and children, and therefore he was guilty of murder.

"I will not by my vote appropriate a single dollar to honor the memory of a man whom I believe a murderer. I therefore vote 'no.' "

As soon as the roll call was completed, Davis of Kiowa, moved that the attacks be expunged from the record, but the motion failed and the attacks stand.

(See also John Brown, of Ossawatomie, by Hill Peebles Wilson, edition of 1913).

. WHY THE SOUTH DEMANDS CORRECTED TEXT BOOKS:

FIRST:

>   Because history as now written will condemn the South to infamy.

SECOND:

>   Because the reference books now in the public libraries will condemn the South to infamy.

THIRD:

>   As long as these falsehoods remain within reach of the student all teaching to the contrary will be in vain.

FOURTH:

>   Because the omissions now in history do the South greater injustice than the commissions of history. (See pp. 112, 113).

THE SOUTH AS REPRESENTED IN HISTORY AND LITERATURE TODAY.

DAVIDSON'S *History* says:

>   "The Jamestown Colonists were vicious idlers and jail birds picked up on the streets of London.
>   "Side by side the two civilizations had grown up in America—the one dedicated to progress had kept up with the spirit of the age—the other a landed aristocracy ·with slavery as the chief excuse for its existence."

MONTGOMERY'S *History* says:

>   "Georgia was settled by filthy, ragged, dirty prisoners taken from the *"Debtors Prison"* by Oglethorpe."

THE BRITISH ENCYCLOPEDIA says:

>   "North Carolina was a refuge for the lawless and adventurous."
>   "The immigration to Virginia consisted of boys and girls seized in the streets of London and shipped as felons."

New Twentieth Century Edition of ENCYCLOPEDIA BRITANNICA, page 360, American Literature:

>   "Like the Spartan marshaling his helots, the Southern planter lounging among his slaves was made dead to art by a paralyzing sense known as his own superiority."
>   "In the world of letters, at least, the ·Southern States shone by reflected light."

"Since the Revolution the few thinkers born South of Mason and Dixon line—outnumbered by those belonging to the single State of Massachusetts—have migrated to New York or Boston for a university training."

"If the negroes were good for food, the probability is that the power of destroying their lives would be enjoyed by their Southern owners as fully as it is over the lives of their cattle.

"Negroes are looked on only as brutes! They are fed or kept hungry; clothed or kept naked, beaten and turned out to the fury of the elements, with as little remorse as if they were beasts of the field."—*Pelham Papers.*

LODGE'S *"History of the Early Colonies":*

"The life of the Southern women was very monotonous— they had few advantages, and were unequal to any refined conversation. They were fond of dancing but showed great want of taste or elegance and seldom appeared with grace. At the close of the evening it was their custom to dance jigs which custom they borrowed from the negroes."

"Family Life in Virginia," p. 344:

"A girl of good fortune or of good reputation is a thing scarce in these parts—for they have no established laws and very little of the Gospel."

HENRY CABOT LODGE'S *"History of the Early Colonies,"* p. 154:

"The negroes in South Carolina were helplessly degraded, rarely baptized or married, lived like animals, their condition of complete barbarism—the slaves were grievously overworked."

HENRY CABOT LODGE'S *"History of the Early Colonies":*

"The Southern man on his plantation drinks a julep made of rum, water and sugar, very strong; rides over his plantation, returns and takes his toddy, lies down to sleep with two negroes to fan him, one at his head and one at his feet; rises for dinner, takes his toddy again and continues to take his toddy all afternoon, then eats his supper and retires for the night."

RICHARD HILDRETH:

"The typical Southern planter is a tall, raw-boned individual, clad in a black frock coat, with his trousers tucked into high-top boots. On his head is a wide brimmed slouch hat, and his heels are adorned with large rowelled spurs. He wears a turn-down collar and a flowing black tie. His hair is long and his beard is worn as a goatee. He carries a whip in his right hand and is accompanied by a dog supposed to be fresh from the chase of a runaway slave.''

Read in striking contrast Bill Arp's description of a Southern gentleman, and Thomas Nelson Page's ''*The Gentleman of the Black Stock.*''

''*Smart Set,*'' New York, February, 1920:

> ''The Southern people know nothing of music or the drama, and view a public library merely as something to be vigorously censored. Lynching is the only public amusement that they never denounce.''

MEANS OF ENFORCING THE MASTER'S EMPIRE.

HILDRETH'S ''*Despotism in America,*'' p. 41:

> The slave late in coming from the field—receives twenty lashes.
>
> ''The slave that is idle—thirty lashes.
>
> ''The slave that disobeys—forty lashes.
>
> ''The slave that destroys property—fifty lashes.
>
> ''The slave that lies—sixty lashes.
>
> ''The slave that is suspected of theft—seventy lashes.
>
> ''The slave that is insolent—eighty lashes.
>
> ''The slave that is insubordinate—one hundred lashes.
>
> ''If he ventures to run away he is pursued by men and dogs, disabled by small shot, and as soon as he is caught, he is flogged till he faints, then worked in chains, locked up every night, and kept on half allowance, till his spirits are broken, and he becomes contented and obedient. Should he offer resistance he is either shot ,stabbed, beat to the ground with a club, and if not killed he is subjected to all sorts of discipline and flogged every night for thirty days in succession. This is a specimen of discipline in plantation management.''

This book from which these extracts are taken is in one of the leading libraries in the State of Georgia. The effect it has had, possibly, on many of Georgia's boys is to make them rank abolitionists?

RICHARD HILDRETH, ''*Despotism in America,*'' p. 45:

> ''The Bible has been proscribed at the South, as an incendiary publication; a book not fit for slaves to read or hear. In some parts of the country the catechism is looked upon with almost equal suspicion: and many masters forbid their slaves to hear any preacher, black or white, since they consider religion upon the plantation as quite out of place, a thing dangerous to the master's authority, and therefore not to be endured in the slave.''

RICHARD HILDRETH, *"Despotism in America,"* p. 71:

"The slaves are regarded not merely as animals, but as animals of the wildest and most ferocious character. They are thought to be like tigers, trained to draw the plough, whom nothing but fear, the whip, and constant watchfulness, keep at all in subjection, and who if left to themselves would quickly recover their savage natures, and find no enjoyment except to reek in blood."

LODGE'S *"History of the Early Colonies"*:

"The strength of Virginia really resided in the Puritan blood which was in their midst.

"For a century Virginia lay in a state of torpor.

"Aversion to towns was very great, but due to indolence, jealousy, and selfishness.

"Neither arts nor letters flourished. Every man taught his own children according to his ability.

"Intellectual amusements were wanting in Maryland. Education had never been an object of interest.

"The slaves of the South were not allowed to have a dog. They were coarsely clothed and fed upon meal and water sweetened with molasses and even punished with barbarity."

"The planters looked upon themselves as different clay from the rest of the community; they had the virtues and vices of an aristocracy. They were neither enterprising nor inventive."

In history the slaveholder of the South has been so maligned because he separated the mother and child on the block. This contrast is striking.

Taken from the Massachusetts Historical Collections, Vol. IV., p. 200, is an advertisement that appeared in *The Continental Journal*, Boston, Mass., March 1, 1781:

"A likely negro wench 19 years old with a child six months of age to be sold *together* or *apart*."

Then a notice that appeared in a newspaper in New Orleans at a later date:

"The Cyclopedia of Political Slavery," Vol. III., p. 733:

"Mr. Hunter was fined $1,000 for separating a mother and child, and compelled to forfeit by the Louisiana law six of his slaves."

LODGE'S *History:*

"If a Bible should be left in a negro cabin, the colporteur would be ushered to Heaven from the lowest limb of a tree on the nearest hill."

"Unless the white race amalgamate with the black, the white will wither from the face of the earth."

When war was threatened in 1861 it was said:

"There can be no war for the cowards of the South would run at the sight of brave soldiers from New England."

An Ohio Suffragist said:

"In the cotton mills of Georgia they work little children from four years up, sending them to and from the mills by rail in an old box car huddled like so many pigs. When the cotton season is over, they are taken to New Jersey and worked in the cranberry fields."

"*The Evening Sun*," Baltimore, Md., Nov. 17, 1919:

"No really first rate woman or man, in any field of endeavor lives in Georgia or has ever lived there. The State has never produced a statesman, a politician, a philosopher, a writer, an artist, or any one who has ever achieved fame. No civilized men and women anywhere; the State is utterly without value."

Lossing's "*History Concerning Robert E. Lee*," Vol. V., Chap. 116, p. 1483:

"The Confederates gained much strength by the defection of Colonel Robert E. Lee of the National Army, who espoused their cause. He lingered in Washington City for a week after the evacuation of Fort Sumter; and when he had drawn from General Scott (who had the most implicit confidence in Lee's honor) all information possible concerning the plans, and resources of the government to be employed in suppressing the rebellion, he resigned his commission (April 20, 1861), deserted his flag, went to Richmond, was appointed commander-in-chief of the military forces of Virginia and *made* war upon the government he had solemnly sworn to support and defend. He gave to its enemies the advantages of his knowledge of the government secrets, and his skill as an engineer. He had kept up a correspondence with those enemies while professing to be loyal to his government; and when that enemy offered him an exalted position, he joined them and worked faithfully for them."

"*The Official History of Suffrage*" says:

"General Lee drove his daughter, Anne Carter, from Arlington as an outcast, because she remained true to the Union. Anne died the third year of the war homeless, with no relative near, dependent for care and nursing and consolation in her last hours upon the kindly services of an old colored woman.''

"The speech of John Brown at Charlestown and the speech of Abraham Lincoln at Gettysburg are the two best specimens of eloquence which we have had in this country.''

"Boys of '61," Coffin, p. 446

"That secession was inaugurated without cause must ever be the verdict of history.''

"I called upon some of my female friends. I knew they were secessionists, but did not think they were so utterly corrupt as I find them to be.'' (p. 29).

"The slaves were the true, loyal men of the South. They did what they could to put down the Rebellion.'' (p. 518).

"Mason, the lordly senator, and Governor Letcher, the drunken executive of the State (Virginia), addressed the crowd fired to a burning heat of madness by passion and whiskey.'' (p. 520).

"Twelve thousand, nine hundred and ninety graves are numbered on the neighboring hillside, murdered by Jeff Davis, Robert E. Lee, James Seddon, John C. Breckenridge—murdered with premeditated design.'' (p. 411).

In J. G. HOLLAND's *"Life of Abraham Lincoln,"* is found on page 293:

"The rebellion was conceived in perjury, brought forth in violence, cradled in ignorance, and reared upon spoils. It never had an apology for its existence that will be entertained for a moment at the bar of history. It was never anything from its birth to its death but a crime—a crime against Christianity, a crime against patriotism, a crime against civilization, a crime against progress, a crime against personal and political honor, a crime against the people of the North who had to put it down, a crime against God to whom they blasphemously appealed for aid.''

J. G. HOLLAND again says:

"The South was prepared for war—nearly all Southern forts had been seized. . The Northern arsenals had been robbed by that miscreant, Floyd. The South refused to pay the debts due the North. The mails were ransacked so that the government could reach neither friends nor foes. She had been drilling men and instructing officers for years. They knew there were not arms enough in the North to overcome them. Maryland, a slaveholding State, had one out of five for rebellion.''

"The British Weekly":

"In the American Civil War the Southern Confederate

women wore personal ornaments made of the bones of their unburied foes. They starved their prisoners and took their scalps for trophies.''

James Russell Lowell was given as authority for this statement.

MR. JAMES RUSSELL LOWELL also said:

''I do not find that the cuticular aristocracy of the South has added anything to the requirements of civilization except the carrying of bowie knives and the chewing of tobacco—a high-toned Southern gentleman being commonly not only quad-rumanous but quid-ruminant.''

MUZZEY'S ''History of the American People'' says:

''The cause for which the Confederate soldier fought was an unworthy cause and should have been defeated.''

''It is impossible for the student of history today to feel otherwise than that the cause for which the South fought was unworthy.''

''The Confederacy was now placed before the civilized world in its true light as the champion of the detested institution of slavery.''—Davidson.

THE ''Chicago Tribune'' says:

The South is half educated, a region of illiteracy, blatant self-righteousness, cruelty and violence.''

CHAMPION'S ''War of the Union,'' p. 316:

''A sort of poetic justice impelled the Federals to send a brigade of colored troops to take possession of Richmond.''

WILLIAM & MARY ''Quarterly,'' Oct. 1918, pp. 82, 83:

'' 'Necessity knows no law,' and 'to save the lives of the gallant men who had so long held Fort Sumter against an overwhelming force of heartless traitors and wicked and unprincipled rebels whose treason has been steeped in fraud and theft vulgarly known as 'Southern Chivalry,' the President of the United States (Abraham Lincoln) in the discharge of a duty to humanity has signed the order for the evacuation of Fort Sumter.''

The Librarian in Pueblo, Colorado, said that ''The Clansman,'' by Thomas Dixon, was too indecent to be read, so ordered all books by Dixon to be taken out of the Library and extra copies of ''Uncle Tom's Cabin'' placed there.

''The New York World,'' Dec. 1919:

''The next President will be a Republican, with a Republican House and Senate, and the Southern States will

be mere provinces. Had it not been for Northern Democrats the Southern States would as yet be as conquered
provinces without influence at Washington.''

XIX.

The Villification of Jefferson Davis Was Necessary to Make the Glorification of Abraham Lincoln More Effective.

AUTHORITY:

"Harper's Weekly," June, 1865:

"The murder of President Lincoln furnished the final
proof of the ghastly spirit of the rebellion. Davis inspired
the murder of Lincoln."

CHENEY's *"History of the Civil War,"* p. 359:

"Poor Jeff Davis began to feel like a wandering Jew—a
price was put on his head. He dared rest nowhere for fear
of meeting the fate of a traitor—afraid to risk an interview with Sherman and not daring to wait for Johnston's
surrender, he fled to Charlotte."

"New York Tribune," 1861:

"The hanging of traitors is sure to begin before the
month is over. The nations of Europe may rest assured
that Jeff Davis will be swinging from the battlements of
Washington at least by the Fourth of July. We spit upon
a later and longer deferred justice."

"The Story of a Great March," Major George W. Nichols:

"The failure of Jeff Davis has brought down on him the
hatred and abuse of his own people. Were he here today
nothing but execration would have been showered uon him.''

"Harper's Weekly," June 17, 1865:

"Davis is as guilty of Lincoln's murder as Booth. Davis
was conspicuous for every extreme of ferocity, inhumanity
and malignity. He was responsible for untold and unim-
aginable cruelties practiced on loyal citizens in the South."

THADDEUS STEVENS, House of Congress, March 19, 1867:

"While I would not be bloody-minded, yet if I had my
way I would long ago have organized a military tribunal
under military power and I would have put Jefferson Davis
and all the members of the Cabinet on trial for the mur-
ders at Andersonville. Jefferson Davis murdered a
thousand men, robbed a thousand widows and orphans, and
burned down a thousand homes."

"Harper's Weekly":

"If it seems too incredible to be true that rebel leaders were guilty of Lincoln's assassination, it must be remembered that Lincoln's murder is no more atrocious than many crimes of which Davis is notoriously guilty."

JOHN FORNEY, Clerk of the Senate—*Washington Chronicle:*

"The judiciary has ample evidence of Davis' guilt of Lincoln's murder, and of the murder of our soldiers in prison."

BOUTWELL, of Massachusetts, introduced the following resolution in Congress:

"*Be* it *Resolved,* That Jefferson Davis shall be held and tried on the charge of killing prisoners and murdering Abraham Lincoln."

"Jefferson Davis wrote a history of the struggle but it was full of prejudice."

CHENEY'S *"History,"* p. 539:

"Davis had in his possession $100,000 in gold belonging to the Confederate Government."

"He was arrested near Macon disguised as a woman, with a shawl over his head and carrying a tin pail."

XX.

Some of the Omissions of History.

"At the First Battle of Bull Run raw, untrained Union soldiers were defeated by well-trained Confederate soldiers. Congress, however, and the President were only nerved by this defeat to prepare for a bigger war."

What should have been there was what an eye witness—the War Correspondent, Edmund Clarence Stedman—saw and put in the columns of *"The New York World":*

"I was with the brave Captain Alexander when the sudden reverse came. 'What does it all mean?' I asked.

" 'It means defeat,' was his reply. 'We are beaten. It is a shameful, cowardly retreat.'

" 'Hold up, men!' he shouted. 'Don't be such cowards,' but on they rushed.

"I saw officers with leaves and eagles on their shoulder straps, majors and colonels who had deserted their commands, galloping as for dear life.

"What a scene! How terrific the onset of that tumultous retreat! Who ever saw such a flight? Who ever saw a more shameful abandonment of munitions gathered at such vast expense? Thousands of muskets strewed the route. The regular cavalry—I say it to their shame—joined in the melee adding to its terrors—for they rode down footmen without mercy. Enough supplies were captured for a week's feast of thanksgiving. The rout of the Federal Army was complete."—"*Great Epochs of American History,*" Vol. VIII.

Another omission of history is the description of the *Merrimac* (Virginia) and the *Monitor*.

History records "an indecisive victory between the *Monitor* and *Virginia*. The *Virginia* finally withdrew up the Elizabeth River."

The following is the truth given by those on the *Virginia* and corroborated by the testimony of the English and French men-of-war anchored at Hampton Roads:

"It was April before the *Merrimac* (Virginia) had completed some alterations, then she steamed down to Hampton Roads under Commodore Tatnall to engage and capture the *Monitor*. She was afraid to go too close to shallow water, but three times she dared and challenged the *Monitor* to come out and fight. Not even the capture of two brigs and a schooner, the *Thomas Jefferson* and the hoising of the Confederate flags on these captured ships, which must have been a humiliation to her, would tempt the *Monitor* to move. Had she taken the dare, she would undoubtedly have been captured and she knew it."

OTHER OMISSIONS OF HISTORY:

The South claims that her best writers are ruled out of a compendium of American Literature and those not literary given prominence.

LITERATURE:

Stedman's *American Literature* gives fifty pages to Walt Whitman and five lines to Henry Timrod.

Richardson gives forty pages to Fenimore Cooper and four pages to William Gilmore Simms, that pioneer of romance.

Pattee, in his *American Literature,* gives page after page to E. P. Roe, and does not mention James Lane Allen.

Houghton, Mifflin & Co., in their *Masterpieces of Literature,* give O'Reilly's prosaic poem, "*The Puritans,*" and does not mention Poe's "*Raven.*"

To read Northern history one would believe that Paul Revere's Ride was the greatest in American history. It does not compare to John Jouett's ride nor Edward Lacy's ride, nor Sam Dale's ride and surely not to Wade Hampton's grandfather's ride of 750 miles in ten days to carry the news of Andrew Jackson's victory at New Orleans. That was a ride of great import in history for New England had already sent her commissioner to say she would *secede* from the Union to join England, but when she heard of the British defeat the papers of secession were not presented.

Lightning Source UK Ltd.
Milton Keynes UK
UKOW01f1006050917
308616UK00007B/781/P